AFRICAN SAINTS
AFRICAN STORIES

African Saints
40 HOLY MEN AND WOMEN
African Stories

CAMILLE LEWIS BROWN, PH.D.

ST. ANTHONY MESSENGER PRESS
Cincinnati, Ohio

Cover design by Constance Wolfer
Cover illustration by ShutterStock / EcoPrint
Cover border textile by ShutterStock / Luba V. Nel
Book design by Jennifer Tibbits

Library of Congress Cataloging-in-Publication Data

Brown, Camille Lewis.
African Saints, African stories : 40 holy men and women / Camille Lewis Brown.
p. cm.
Includes bibliographical references and index.
ISBN 978-0-86716-805-1 (pbk. : alk. paper) 1. Christian saints—Africa—Biography. I. Title.
BR1700.3.B76 2008
276.0092′2—dc22
[B]

2007048942

ISBN 978-0-86716-805-1

Published by St. Anthony Messenger Press
28 W. Liberty St.
Cincinnati, OH 45202
www.SAMPBooks.org

Printed on acid-free paper
Printed in the United States of America

08 09 10 11 12 5 4 3 2 1

To
Aaron Lewis, Jr.
(1957–2000)
My brother, confidant and friend

Contents

Foreword

It is natural that we search for black presence in church history. There is evidence of African contribution throughout Sacred Scripture, beginning with Genesis 2, where the sources of the Nile River are located, to the deacon Philip's baptism of the Ethiopian official in service to the Nubian queen, Candace, in Acts 8. This latter New Testament passage is popularly understood to be a report of Africa's introduction to the gospel.

Luke, a gentile, author of the third Gospel, looked for the gentiles in Jesus' audience and set out to tailor an account of the Lord's ministry that would emphasize to them that the phenomenon of Christ included them as well. So why shouldn't we want to find black people among Christ's earliest disciples? Why shouldn't we be curious as to whether or not Jesus ever spoke to a black person?

Unlike some in modern society, writers of the ancient world did not always find it necessary to reference people by the color of their skin. This is why we cannot know with certainty whether the fourth-century saint Augustine and his mother, Monica, were Negroid or not, or whether any of the early popes were Negroid and not simply Roman Africans, Roman citizens or Mediterranean people who lived in Africa.

A black person is revealed in the Bible often by his or her name or city or place of origin. This is about as close as we can get to identifying the role of Africans, our ancestors, in the world of the Old Testament and some of the earliest players in Christianity mentioned in the New Testament. Consider these identifiers, for example:

- *Cush* in Hebrew and *Ethiopia* in Greek designate the land and peoples of the upper Nile River from modern southern Egypt into the Sudan. The more indigenous term for this region is *Nubia*. *Ham* is another Hebrew term for the darker-skinned people of antiquity. In Genesis 10 Ham is the son of Noah, whose descendants populate Africa, Canaan and Arabia after the flood. In biblical poetry the name *Ham* is a synonym for Egypt (Psalm 78).

- *Niger* (N-eye-jer) in Latin is the word for "black" used to identify an African by the name of Simeon in Acts 13. Simeon's companion, Lucius, might also be black as indicated by his place of origin, Cyrene. These two men are documented as two of the earliest teachers and prophets in the infant church. The man who was forced to help Jesus carry the cross to the hill of execution, Simon, is also from Cyrene (Matthew 27).

It is not easy determining how deeply African modern-day Egyptians consider themselves save for Egypt being an obvious part, in the corner, of the Dark Continent. The Bible uses the word *Africa* to describe the length of the Nile valley from the deep southern origins of the Nile down to the delta where it empties into the Mediterranean Sea. From the Lower Nile in the north to the Upper Nile in the south, skin color, in the ancient world, varied from brown to copper-brown to black. Furthermore, Egypt, along with Canaan and Arabia, are referred to collectively as Africa by the Genesis accounts of restored humanity after the flood (Genesis 10). Northern Egyptians referred to their southern neighbors as *Nehesi*, which came to mean "the black" or "the Nubian." This same term is found in Exodus 6, referring to the brother of Moses, Aaron's grandson, Phinehas. Moses' wife was a Cushite (Numbers 12).

Skin color bias is, without doubt, more insidious in our modern time than anything that history records of the ancient world. Even the ancient institution of slavery was not focused so much on skin color or race but rather on any people subjugated from anywhere, most often following conquest. Ancient slavery consumed quite a variety of different peoples.

Many of the early monks and hermits were black men. Church history would demonstrate that North Africa proved prominent as a site of several of the early church councils. So the participation of black people in salvation history and early church history is definite and impressive. Blacks were there from the beginning.

It is equally natural to search for black presence among the recognized saints of the Catholic church. For in so doing we trace pride in the contribution of people who hail from the Dark Continent with our faith and heritage.

We must be careful whom from ancient history we label black and African. The gospel was not taken to the sub-Saharan regions of black Africa largely until the nineteenth century, when missionary activity by Europeans was strongest. In the early centuries North Africa was colonized by Mediterranean peoples whose lineage was largely Roman, Greek or mixed.

If we are talking about African saints, we are talking about a host of holy men and women who lived in those first three to five centuries of the faith and who were black Africans, Romans, Greeks or Mediterranean-Caucasian colonizers.

If we are talking exclusively of black saints, we are talking about a restricted group of peoples from regions of black Africa, including Egypt, who are those of Negroid descent like Moses the Black and, perhaps, Antony of Egypt, the founder of Christian monasticism.

To say there have been black popes is next to impossible to establish with certainty. We know there have been none in modern times. From evidence that we have, the early popes who had origins in Africa seem to have been of Roman, Greek or Mediterranean origin and who lived in Rome's colonized regions of North Africa, similar to white Europeans who colonized South Africa in our time. In other words, we need evidence that Pope Saint Gelasius (492–496) was a black man and not simply a white African. The problem is the same, as cited earlier, with saints like Perpetua (d. 203); her slave who was martyred with her, Felicitas, may well have been a black slave. Augustine (354–430) and his mother Monica (331–387): Were they black or Algerian? Clearer evidence is needed. Regardless, their stories are included in this book, for they provide examples of perseverance in faith and holiness.

Benedictine monk and historian Cyprian Davis, O.S.B., in his celebrated book *The History of Black Catholics in the United States,* writes, "the black presence in the early Church in North Africa and Europe may be a shadowy one, its extent may be measured more by legend than by verifiable data, but the reality of this presence is undeniable...."[1]

Most Reverend Joseph N. Perry
Auxiliary Bishop of Chicago

Acknowledgments

"I have given everything to my master: He will take care of me."
—Saint Josephine Bakhita

I must first thank the good Lord for his involvement in this project. The journey to completion was a bit rocky, but I always prayed and asked these great saints to be with me. Sometimes I was sure that Satan tried to stop the progress of this text, but God prevailed, as God always does. So I say thank you, Lord.

So many others were interested in this work, and I know that their support added to this final text. First, I must say thank you to my pastor, Monsignor Federico Britto. I know that you were praying for me as you did not seem to mind my endless questions about the material. God will bless you abundantly for your generosity to this humble servant. Thanks also to my wonderful friend, Sister Suzanne Neisser, R.S.M., whose constant prayers, vision and suggestions created a positive (and quiet) environment for me to commune with the saints. I honestly must also thank Mr. James Watson for his technological assistance in the final hours of polishing up this work.

To the prayerful folks at St. Cyprian Parish, God heard your prayers for me, so thanks. Please know that I pray for you, too! I would be remiss if I forgot to express my gratitude to my recent Religious Studies 214 ("African Saints, African-American Holy Men and Women") class. You were so fabulous about reading and evaluating the sample chapters. I read every word of every survey. Your comments helped to polish the overall text. The saints are definitely with you!

Throughout this process I have from time to time required special research help. I am happy to say thank you to Jim Humble and Todd Wilmot from the St. Charles Borromeo Seminary library. You guys were so patient and kind to me. You were always willing to help me find research material and assist me with reference issues. You didn't have to spend so much time with me, but I'm glad you did. Thanks also to the seminary's Religious Studies Division for asking me to design the African Saints course so many years ago. The research required for this course piqued my interest in just how many African saints were honored in the Catholic church.

Every once in a while I encounter friends who will be my friends forever. To all of my friends in Africa who gently assisted with this project, I say thank you. Really, to properly study African saints, one should visit the continent, if possible.

This book became a reality because Ms. Valerie Washington, the Executive Director of the National Black Catholic Congress, asked me to write an article on African saints. After reading this article, those at St. Anthony Messenger Press liked the idea so much that they wanted a book. Much thanks to Ms. Washington and a big thank-you to everyone at St. Anthony Messenger Press for their interest in these saints.

Introduction

In great despair and sometimes great happiness, we call upon these fine men and women of the church, these who have reached the highest pinnacle of the altar. We call on them as saints of the universal church. Throughout the centuries of Catholicism it can seem that the vision of saintly people of color has been lost. Evidence of this lays herein as few Catholics, black or white, are aware of the multitude of African saints. Most Catholics know about Saint Martin de Porres from Lima, Peru, or mistakenly believe that Saint Peter Claver was of African descent, as he served and evangelized the slaves. Though they were certainly great men of their time and a gift to holy mother church, identifying them as the only African saints is an academic and spiritual error.

I have steadily attempted to nurture a transformation in these views throughout the past ten years that I have been teaching the course entitled "The History of Black Catholics in the United States" at St. Charles Borromeo Seminary in Wynnewood, Pennsylvania. This course includes saints and other holy men and women of African descent. Preparation for the teaching of this course opened my eyes to the concept of black and African saints and their massive effect and contributions to the church. Prior to this point I, too, only knew about a limited number of saints from the continent of Africa. My passion for the saints grew as the years of teaching mounted, discussions on the topic became lengthier and more involved. By the year 2000 I knew that traveling throughout Africa was key to confirming the rich faith heritage of the lives of African saints. As I visited countries, I had the pleasure of asking African Catholics about their saints. This firsthand knowledge enriched my own faith experience and stoked the fire of my passion to know more about the saints of Africa. Even today, as I travel to Africa every year, I continue to ask about the saints.

Three years ago the seminary asked me to design and teach a course on the African saints. This invitation truly was an awakening of sorts because now the doors were opened to conduct research and to devote entire class sessions to African saints. Each new class presents a new opportunity to invite students on this journey with me as I walk with the saints and other holy men and women of African descent.

As I began this text, my African saint count was up to 704, but now I must report that the actual number is beyond measure. There is evidence in the text to reveal that many, many groups and companions were martyred from the continent of Africa, thus making it impossible to pinpoint an exact number. But just in case you are a saint counter, please see the litany at the book's end.

This is a book designed for personal prayer, reflection and possible retreat time, but basically it is a text for all of us to commune with the saints. This is an opportunity to touch the lives, as it were, of ordinary men and women, just like us, who simply tried to live the gospel.

African Saints, African Stories was also written to enhance school curricula (a great classroom companion for students), to energize sacramental preparations and to revitalize Bible study groups, black history programs and parish council meetings. It also makes a great gift. Whoever receives this book will delight and remain in awe over this version of the lives of the saints.

This book includes four parts in each of its forty chapters. These sections guide you with a brief biography of each holy person, a relevant passage from Scripture, a brief prayer and a few reflection questions. The expected goal of such an arrangement was that each reader could apply the material in his or her own way. It should be noted here that, in the tradition of the Catholic faith, by praying "to" these saints we are not worshiping them, but calling upon them, asking them to pray for us as we are praying for them, seeking their intercession in the great communion of saints. As author Carolyn Trickey-Bapty in her book *Martyrs and Miracles* states, "The Roman Catholic church teaches that God gives the saints the ability to hear and see our needs. So we ask saints for guidance or help by calling upon them during prayer. Though saints serve as a communication link between us and God, our prayers to saints do not replace our prayers to God."[2]

The first thirty chapters of this book address holy men and women that the church has already officially recognized as a saint, blessed or venerable. Put simply, once a local and an official church investigation into the life of a person particularly holy and virtuous has taken place, the pope can declare the person venerable. If the venerable person was a martyr, the pope can then beatify this person, declaring him or her blessed. If not a martyr, a miracle must be attributed to the person before he or she can be declared blessed. To be canonized a saint, an additional miracle must be attributed to the person.

The final ten chapters of this book celebrate the lives of men and women who have contributed to the Catholic church but remain without one of these titles. They are the "Saints in Waiting," heroes already in God's presence, members of the communion of saints, but unclassified as such by the church.

In their ordinary states, these extraordinary saintly people emerged. It is my hope that your prayer experience will be enriched and that whatever trials you are undergoing, God will send help soon. I hope the opportunity for this positive experience will be a rewarding one for all who make this journey with the African saints. You are humbly invited to walk into the heart of this book as ordinary men and women of the church. Here you will find that these holy men and women led lives similar to your own. They had families, church responsibilities, dreams, fears and hopes for the future. But, mostly, they had faith in the promises of Christ.

As Christians committed to the universal church, the heroes of this text show us how to remain faithful despite struggles, disappointments and setbacks. They continue to show us how to embrace the gospel in our ordinary day-to-day lives. This is a remarkable opportunity for all of us to see examples of Christianity in action. Here, at the heart of the book, is a chance for each of us to be spiritually charged and enriched by our heroes.

Finally, I hope that the wonderful legacy of these Catholic saints inspire all readers as they learn about the contributions of people of color. Young people and those more seasoned can know more of their rich history as members of the universal church. To know this historical part of our faith means that you can proudly embrace it, care for it, nurture it and hold onto it for the rest of your days. As I invite you to call upon the African saints, feel free to notice which ones make you say, "Wow!"

Part One
Saints, Blesseds and Venerables

Men and Women for Others

Although countless numbers of martyrs come from the city of Alexandria, the martyrs of the Alexandrian plague are significant, as these were Christians in hiding from the anti-Christian persecutions imposed by the emperors Valerian and Decius in the third century. They came out of hiding during the height of the plague to nurse the sick and bury the dead. These martyrs are not remembered individually by name because they perished in groups: some from the plague that engulfed the city, some from the tortures that they experienced once captured by the authorities.

The sacrifice of these martyrs was desperately needed as Alexandria was already under siege by famine and violence. The plague and persecutions added to this indignity. *Butler's Lives of the Saints* describes this violent, horrific period:

> Corpses lay unburied, and the air was laden with infection, mingled with pestilential vapours from the Nile. The living appeared wild with terror, and the fear of death rendered the pagan citizens cruel to their nearest relations; as soon as anyone was known to have caught the infection, his friends fled from him: the bodies of those not yet dead were thrown into the streets and abandoned.[3]

But as Jesus tells us, "No one has greater love than this, to lay down one's life for one's friends" (John 15:13). This was the spirit that embraced the martyrs of Alexandria, as they risked their own lives for those in need.

I

Alexandrian Plague Martyrs and Other African Martyrs

=====

Comforters of the Sick and Dying

===

d. 257

Feast Day
February 28

=

Most of the brethren were prodigal in their love and brotherly kindness. They supported one another, visited the sick fearlessly, and looked after them without stint, serving them in Christ. They were happy to die with them, bearing their neighbours' burdens and taking their disease and pain on themselves, even to the death which they caught from them....

With their own bare hands, they closed the eyes and mouths of the saints; they carried their bodies away and laid them out; they embraced and kissed them, washed them and put on their grave-clothes.[4]

In this gentle way the martyrs of the Alexandrian plague humbly served their community members, and sometimes they needed other neighbors to serve them in the same way, gently ushering their souls home to the Lord.

OTHER ALEXANDRIAN MARTYRS

d. 257: A group of Christians, according to Saint Dionysius of Alexandria, suffered hideous tortures and truly gruesome acts at the hands of their Roman captors. Feast day: August 10.

d. 342: Christians slain by Arian pagans on Good Friday. Saint Athanasius described this martyrdom in his writings. Feast day: March 21.

d. 356: Christians martyred while celebrating Mass by a Roman official. Feast day: January 28.

d. 372: Christians slain when Arian elements in the city attacked Saint Athanasius for his opposition to a heresy. Feast day: May 13.

d. 390: Christians attacked by pagan worshipers of the god Serapis. When the Christians refused to take part in the ritual of Serapis, they were attacked by a mob and put to death. Feast day: March 17.

OTHER AFRICAN MARTYRS

There are countless numbers of martyrs from the continent of Africa whose names and dates have been lost. The collective name given to the martyrs who died for the faith is *Mauretania Tingitana* (or Africa Latina), which was the name for a Roman province of northwestern Africa. The martyrs vary according to year and feast day.

date unknown: Two hundred and twenty Christians of Africa whose deaths were not detailed to any extent. Feast day: October 16.

date unknown: A group of Christians, numbering between one and two hundred; no details of their deaths have survived. Feast day: October 30.

date unknown: A group called the *Martryes Massylitani* was put to death in Masyla in North Africa. The fourth-century Latin poet Prudentius wrote a hymn in their honor. Feast day: April 9.

d. ca. 210: Christian men and women died in the persecution under Emperor Septimius Severus (r. 193–211). They were burned at the stake. Feast day: January 6.

d. ca. 303: A group of martyrs known as "the Guardians of the Holy Scriptures" were Christians who refused to turn over the sacred Christian books to the authorities to be burned. Several "Guardians" groups were killed. Saint Augustine had high praise for those in Nicomedia. Feast day: February 11.

d. 459: A large group of Christians put to death by the Arian King Geiseric of the Vandals (r. 428–477). As they refused to abjure the orthodox faith, Geiseric had them slain at a celebration of the Eucharist on Easter Sunday. A lector was shot by an arrow through the throat while chanting the Alleluia verse. Feast day: April 5.

d. 482: Christian women put to death by the Vandal King Huneric (r. 477–484) for refusing to accept Arian Christianity. Feast day: December 16.

SCRIPTURE

This is my commandment, that you love one another as I have loved you. No one has greater love than this, to lay down one's life for one's friends. You are my friends if you do what I command you. I do not call you servants any longer, because the servant does not know what the master is doing; but I have called you friends, because I have made known to you everything that I have heard from my Father. You did not choose me but I chose you. And I appointed you to go and bear fruit, fruit that will last, so that the Father will give you whatever you ask him in my name. I am giving you these commands so that you may love one another. (John 15:12–17)

PRAYER

Dear Alexandrian Martyrs, servants to all, how did you sacrifice yourselves so willingly? Though hidden from persecution, you revealed yourselves to assist the suffering and dead of Alexandria. You were committed to acts of mercy and Christian charity by comforting the sick and burying the dead. Truly, you laid down your lives for others. In all of your selfless acts, you saw Christ in your neighbor. Martyrs of Alexandria, pray for us that we might see Christ in our neighbor, too. Amen.

REFLECTION

In your twenty-first–century community how can you lay down your life for others? As violence, abuse and persecution engulf your community and the communities around you, how can you see Christ in your neighbor?

The Solitary Saint

Saint Antony willingly entered a solitary life as he sold everything that he had, entrusted the care of his sister to virgins in his village and lived for a period inside a tomb in a cemetery. One account of Antony describes a man raised by wealthy Christian parents. Upon their deaths Antony heard the voice of God calling him to a more disciplined life. Another saga portrays Antony being raised by peasant parents who nurtured their children in Christianity. Whichever story is accurate, we know that at some point Antony began to live a monastic life in the desert outside Thebes in Egypt. Solitude was central to his existence for the remainder of his life.

There is often some confusion as to why Antony is referred to as the founder of Christian monasticism, a way of life that involves living in seclusion from the world. Evidence suggests that Antony was not the first monk. There were many who rejected all wealth and human relations to embrace a life of solitude and prayer. In fact, the custom of the time was to live in the desert near one's own village. This is exactly what Antony did near Thebes. The reason that this holy man inherited this title is that he further defined what is expected in the monastic life. Antony's sayings, a few of which are listed below, call others to experience a life devoted to prayer.

> Somebody asked Antony, "What shall I do in order to please God?" He replied, "Do what I tell you, which is this: wherever you go, keep God in mind; whatever you do, follow the example of holy Scripture; wherever you are, stay there and do not move

2

Saint Antony of Egypt
=====
Founder of Christian
Monasticism

===

251–356
Feast Day
January 17

=

away in a hurry. If you keep to these guide-lines, you will be saved."[5]

Pambo said to Antony, "What shall I do?" Antony said, "Do not trust in your own righteousness. Do not go on sorrowing over a deed that is past. Keep your tongue and your belly under control."[6]

Those who renounce the world but want to keep their money are attacked in that way by demons and torn in pieces.[7]

Some wear out their bodies by fasting; but because they have no discretion this only puts them further away from God.[8]

Our great work is to lay the blame for our sins upon ourselves before God, and to expect to be tempted to our last breath.[9]

His insights into the souls of humanity were indeed unusual and often caused men of his time to seek him out for his guidance. Antony was also known to have had at least one vision of Christ and was constantly tormented by the devil. Once when the devil beat him, Antony "cried out: Here I am; what do you want? Nothing can separate me from my Lord Jesus Christ. He frightened the devil away by making the sign of the cross. Then Christ appeared to him."[10]

Antony's years of monastic life lasted until the year 356 when this saintly monk returned to his creator at the age of 105. Throughout his years of torment, fasting, labor and solitude, Antony continued to exude happiness and peace and extend charity to all who saw him. During his long years he acted as a spiritual guide, was a visionary, opened monasteries and performed many miracles. Often his great friend Saint Athanasius was at his side to witness God's special blessings on Saint Antony, the founder of Christian monasticism.

SCRIPTURE

[T]o sit alone in silence
> when the Lord has imposed it,
to put one's mouth to the dust
> (there may yet be hope),
to give one's cheek to the smiter,
> and be filled with insults. (Lamentations 3:28–30)

PRAYER

Dear Saint Antony, in your silence you heard the precious voice of Jesus. Always in prayer, always sacrificing human contact in favor of isolation, performing penance and prayer, you allowed little for yourself, saving only your interest in spreading the gospel through spiritual experiences. Those of your time so loved you that you were often sought after for advice and kindness. In your efforts, you remained a champion for church doctrine and a friend to those seeking spiritual growth. Saint Antony, stretch out your hand and touch us in some way so that we see the importance of spiritual growth and dedication to our church. Amen.

REFLECTION

How can you determine when you should speak up and when you should remain silent? Is silence always golden?

Saint of Redemption

Saint Augustine, the great doctor of the church, did not have such an illustrious beginning. His mother, Saint Monica, was a devoted Catholic woman, but his father, Patricius, was a pagan, a womanizer and an abusive father and husband. While Monica remained diligent in presenting the faith to their three children, Patricius rejected baptism and often requested some task from Monica just when it was time for Mass or another faith-centered obligation.

As for Augustine, his mother wanted him to become a Christian, but his father forced the idea of his son becoming a man of learning. This desire set the stage for Augustine's life as a student, teacher and consistent searcher for academic truths. At age nine Augustine was sent away for proper schooling. He returned to his family home in Tagaste (in present-day Algeria) at age sixteen and remained idle for a year after which his parents sent him to the university at Carthage (in present-day Tunisia). The time away gave this young man ample opportunity to explore the moral and immoral aspects of life. While absent from his mother's watchful eyes, Augustine searched for truths to explain humanity and the evils that surround it. As he explored this search for truth, Augustine became attracted to stoicism (the belief that logical thought is reflected or found in cosmic reason), Manichaeanism (the combination of Gnosticism and Buddhism that posits a belief in conflicts between light and dark and matter as dark and evil), Pythagoreanism (the belief that the universe is the result of the combinations of mathematical ratios) and Aristotelianism (a

3

Saint Augustine of Hippo

=====

Sinner, Doctor of the
Church and Saint

===

354–430
Feast Day
August 28

=

belief system that emphasized deduction and investigation of concrete things and situations). These philosphies led Augustine far away from Christianity and the peace of Christ.

Augustine's quest left him easily bored and short tempered with everyone, especially those who failed to understand the seriousness of great learning and higher academic pursuits. Once he began teaching, this attitude prevailed even toward his students who were not ambitious enough academically. Augustine was quick to drop these academic slackers. He only had time for the brilliant and motivated. In his autobiographical work, *Confessions*, Augustine explains his search for truth that eventually led directly to the Risen Lord:

> Lord God of truth, surely the person with a scientific knowledge of nature is not pleasing to you on that ground alone. The person who knows all those matters but is ignorant of you is unhappy. The person who knows you, even if ignorant of natural science, is happy. Indeed the one that knows both you and nature is not on that account happier. You alone are his source of happiness....[11]

If only Augustine knew this lesson sooner in life, he could have avoided many frustrating situations and heartaches for his prayerful mother, Monica. Instead, he moved from one teaching position to another, looking for students bright enough for his instruction and knowledge pure enough to answer his many unanswered dilemmas.

He also found time to participate in criminal activity and sexual misconduct. By his own admission, Augustine was loose in his moral activities. Despite Augustine's sinful ways, he recognized that his mother's voice was God speaking to him, as he realized later in his life:

> Wretch that I am, do I dare to say that you, my God, were silent when in reality I was travelling farther from you? Was it in this sense that you kept silence to me? Then whose words were they but yours which you were chanting in my ears through my mother, your faithful servant? But nothing of that went down into my heart to issue in action. Her concern...was that I should not fall into fornication.... These warnings seemed to me womanish advice.... But they were your warnings and I did not realize it.[12]

As Augustine wandered from city to city, from religious philosophy to religious philosophy, his unhappiness and desire for something more became very apparent to him. His mother witnessed her son's condition and encouraged him to embrace the faith that would bring peace. But Augustine admits that he was seeking one thing:

> I sought an object for my love; I was in love with love.... My hunger was internal, deprived of inward food, that is of you yourself, my God. But that was not the kind of hunger I felt. I was without any desire for incorruptible nourishment.... So my soul was in rotten health. In an ulcerous condition it thrust itself to outward things.... Yet physical things had no soul. Love lay outside their range. To me it was sweet to love and to be loved, the more so if I could enjoy the body of the beloved. I therefore polluted the spring water of friendship with the filth of concupiscence. I muddied its clear stream by the hell of lust, and yet, though foul and immoral, in my excessive vanity, I used to carry on in the manner of an elegant man about town. I rushed headlong into love, by which I was longing to be captured.... My love was returned and in secret I attained the joy that enchains. I was glad to be in bondage, tied with troublesome chains, with the result that I was flogged with the red-hot iron rods of jealousy, suspicion, fear, anger, and contention.[13]

Augustine is speaking of his eventual relationship with a woman (a concubine), to whom he remained faithful for fifteen years and who gave birth to his son, Adeodatus. She was an African woman from a lower position in life than he. This relationship, though it offered Augustine some stability, never offered the opportunity for marriage. Augustine's mother urged him to send the woman back to North Africa, which he did years later, only to find himself living with another woman for two years.

Augustine was on a constant quest for something. At his mother's unending urging, he finally relented and decided to study Scripture but remarked in *Confessions*:

> I therefore decided to give attention to the holy scriptures and to find out what they were like. And this is what met me: something neither open to the proud nor laid bare to mere children; a text

lowly to the beginner but, on further reading, of mountainous difficulty and enveloped in mysteries. I was not in any state to be able to enter into that, or to bow my head to climb its steps. What I am now saying did not then enter my mind when I gave my attention to the scripture. It seemed to me unworthy in comparison with the dignity of Cicero.[14]

Still he moved from Carthage to Rome to Milan, always searching, always knowing that his devoted mother was physically on his heels. This great mother refused to give up on her son and followed him from city to city and prayed for his baptism. Her unending tears and prayers sometimes failed to move her son. She continued to pray for years for his conversion. When Monica pleaded with Augustine to take her on a voyage, he agreed, but sending her to purchase tickets for the voyage home, Augustine bought one ticket and sailed away, leaving his mother on the shore. She remained in Carthage, weeping for her son and begging God to help him.

Augustine's trip to Rome gave him the opportunity to have his conversion experience as recorded in *Confessions*. He tells the tale of being in a garden where he hears a child's voice tell him to "Pick up and read, pick up and read."[15] Immediately he opened Saint Paul's epistles (Romans 13:13–14) and his eyes were opened and he knew truth at last. His life would be forever different, forever good, forever true.

Augustine was baptized, much to his mother's joy, on Holy Saturday night, in April of 387. Augustine speaks of his love and peace, his truth that he has found at last: "Late have I loved you, beauty so old and so new: late have I loved you. And see, you were within and I was the external world.... You were with me, and I was not with you."[16]

Not long after his baptism, Monica died and Augustine's grief could not be consoled. He knew and appreciated her years of suffering on his behalf and, according to Leon Cristiani in his book *Saint Monica and Her Son Augustine*, often said that "his mother had borne him twice: first in the flesh, and afterwards in the spirit.... [T]he second childbirth was perhaps more far painful than the first."[17]

A year after his baptism Augustine returned to Tagaste where he became attracted to the priesthood. Six years later he was ordained. Augustine eventually became the bishop of Hippo, an important see in the Roman Empire. He encountered and vigorously fought against the Manichaeanism, the Donatists (those who were not forgiving of those who had left the church during the emperor Diocletian's persecutions), Pelagianism (the belief, among other things, that original sin did not taint human nature) and Arianism (any belief that contradicted the belief in the Trinity). It is ironic that Augustine used his later years to preach, teach and write against some of the very religious philosophies that he had embraced in his younger life.

After a life spanning seventy-six years, Augustine died. He was blessed in knowing God's mercy and forgiveness as well as God's great and unyielding love for humanity. Augustine began his *Confessions* with this humble appeal,

> "You are great, Lord, and highly to be praised (Ps. 47:2): great is your power and your wisdom is immeasurable" (Ps. 146:5). Man, a little piece of your creation, desires to praise you, a human being "bearing his mortality with him," (2 Cor. 4:10), carrying with him the witness of his sin and the witness that you "resist the proud" (1 Pet. 5:5). Nevertheless, to praise you is the desire of man.... You stir man to take pleasure in praising you, because you have made us for yourself, and our heart is restless until it rests in you.[18]

SCRIPTURE

[T]he night is far gone, the day is near. Let us then lay aside the works of darkness and put on the armor of light; let us live honorably as in the day, not in reveling and drunkenness, not in debauchery and licentiousness, not in quarrelling and jealousy. Instead, put on the Lord Jesus Christ, and make no provision for the flesh, to gratify its desires. (Romans 13:12–14)

PRAYER

Dear Saint Augustine, you led an early life of shame and immoral behavior, causing deep wounds for your mother, Monica. How did she manage to pray for so long and remain hopeful for your conversion? God, in his mercy, never left you. Now we see the great work that you did on behalf of our church, so much you managed to do to help us in our daily lives and in our spiritual growth. We who see your fine example of witnessing to the gospel know that lives and people can change for the better. Help us now to persevere and stay the course toward God's promises, so that we, too, may one day enjoy his sweet presence, for our hearts are restless, too. Amen.

REFLECTION

When are you most willing to open your heart to something new? What does it take for you to accept the change? What are you doing to heal any heartache in your relationships?

The Scapular Saint

While any martyrdom story may be difficult to hear, the martyrdom of Blessed Isidore Bakanja is especially tragic and harsh. His story is that of a young man recently converted and then horrifically beaten because of his Christian faith.

Isidore Bakanja was born sometime in 1880 in what is now the Democratic Republic of the Congo. This was a time of colonization by Europeans eager to make their fortunes in rubber and ivory, which were plentiful in this region of Africa. These Europeans came for financial glory, but neglected to respect the humanity of the indigenous people of the area. In fact, many were cruel and vicious to the Africans who labored on their plantations. Such was the disrespectful environment that Isidore Bakanja encountered working as a mason.

As a result of these cruelties, King Leopold II of Belgium, who controlled the area, asked Pope Leo XII to send missionaries to the Congo. His greatest desire was for the missionaries to calm the hatred of the Europeans for the African populations and eventually perpetuate better relations in the territory. Isidore Bakanja encountered the Trappist priests who came as missionaries and soon professed the Christian faith.

As a member of the Boangi tribe near Mbandaka, a main city near his birthplace, Isidore's name appears on the baptismal records of the missionaries around 1906. He was eager and swift about witnessing to the faith both privately and in public. He often recited the rosary and wore the scapular as a sign of his Christian faith.

4

Blessed Isidore Bakanja
=====
Scapular Martyr

===

1880–1909
Feast Day
August 15

=

On the first plantation where he worked, his supervisor did not object to Isidore's desire to instruct other Africans in the faith. Isidore was very successful with his evangelization efforts; many of his African coworkers became Christians. When his work on the plantation ended, he was assigned to another site in the Congo's interior. There he encountered verbal abuse and anti-Christian sentiments, which would lead to his eventual martyrdom.

But soon Isidore was forced to work under a new Belgian foreman, Van Cauter, known as Longange, who hated Christians. According to author Ann Ball in *Faces of Holiness,* "He often stated that religion was a farce and that priests were 'stupid,' 'ignorant,' and 'zeros.' He called the missionary priests by the pejorative name 'mon père.'"[19] Ball also reports that he referred to Isidore as the "animal of stupid priests."[20]

On one occasion Longange told Isidore to remove his scapular, to stop praying and to end his instruction of the other Africans. When Isidore refused, Longange ripped the scapular from Isidore's neck and savagely beat him. The reports of this attack vary as some give evidence that Longange personally beat Isidore while other men held the catechist down. Another account states Longange tied up Isidore's hands and feet before beating him. Isidore was left for dead in a rubber-processing room, but was discovered by an inspector who tried to heal him.

Some say that Longange ordered the beating and another worker actually delivered the blows while two others held Isidore to the ground. Whatever actually occurred, what remains true is that Isidore's open wounds became infected and did not heal even after medical treatment was administered. Blessed Isidore Bakanja died six months later of his injuries. He was an invalid after the beating, but remained prayerful by reciting his rosary. Even near death he said, "The White man did not like Christians.... Certainly I shall pray for him. When I am in Heaven, I shall pray for him very much."[21]

When Pope John Paul II visited Zaire (now the Democratic Republic of the Congo) in 1980, he told the Catholics there to look to Isidore as a model of strength and courage: "Isidore Bakanja, a true Zairois, a true Christian.... [H]e did not hesitate to offer his life to God, strong in the courage he found in his faith and in the faithful recitation of the Rosary...."[22]

This brother of faith remains an example of true love for God and hope in the resurrection. As a public witness at an unpopular time for Christians, Blessed Isidore Bakanja remained steadfast and should be called upon for intercessory prayers. Pope John Paul II beatified him in 1994.

SCRIPTURE

You are the light of the world. A city built on a hill cannot be hid. No one after lighting a lamp puts it under the bushel basket, but on the lampstand, and it gives light to all in the house. (Matthew 5:14–15)

PRAYER

Blessed Isidore, how strong you were! How truly and unquestionably committed to the faith you were and how strong your convictions! Your model of spreading the Good News continues to inspire us today. When we are concerned about what others will think about us because we are Catholic or Christian, we can look to you, the one who faithfully wore the scapular, a symbol of Christ, our redeemer. When we remain silent about our faith around other Christians at work or at play, we can remember your heroic act of faith. We learn from you that sharing our faith is always a necessary choice. Amen.

REFLECTION

In what ways are you silent about our Catholic faith? Are you strong enough in your faith to defend it if called upon to do so?

Saint of Forgiveness

The story of Saint Josephine Bakhita remains a very moving testament to God's providential hand on all who are called to do God's great work. Although God's work is often found in what some may call menial tasks, all work done in the name of the Lord is work of great magnitude in the eyes of God. With this perspective, we can embrace the life of Bakhita who performed tasks that may not have been great. She did not begin a religious congregation, serve as a missionary to the world or hold high office. She was, according to one of her biographers, simply "a Sister, a slave, sold, bought, resold, unknown in the world, coming from nowhere...!"[23]

Born in the Darfur region of Sudan, Bakhita did not recall her name at birth. She could, however, recall her family's happiness in her very early days of life. When Bakhita was about eight years old, she and a friend set out to search for herbs. They were violently captured and taken away from their home. Early in her captivity, her captors jokingly named her Bakhita, meaning "the lucky one," as a means of confusing and separating the child from everything familiar. Of course, they could not have known the ultimate true luck and blessing she would find in knowing the Lord.

Bakhita's early years of slavery were indeed unlucky as she was tortured, disfigured by tattoos and forced to endure long marches chained and deprived of food and water. Her bondage was marked by constant beatings and the fear of the unknown. She never knew when she would be sold or punished for some unex-

5

Saint Josephine Bakhita

=====

Slave and Religious

===

1869–1947
Feast Day
February 8

=

plained reason. These events imprinted suffering on Bakhita's mind and body. She later said, "Had I known the Lord, during my long slavery, how much less I would have suffered."[24]

Her story is a very emotional one as she was bought and sold five times before being sold to her last owner, who valued Bakhita as a nursemaid to her young daughter in Italy. When her new owner left for Africa, she left Bakhita and the young daughter with the Canossian Sisters of Charity in Venice. Nine months later she returned to Venice to claim the girls, but Bakhita refused to leave. She remarked, "I refused to follow her back to Africa, since my instruction for baptism was not yet completed.... [I]f I had followed her even after receiving baptism, I would not have had the opportunity to practise my new religion. So I decided to stay with the Sisters.... I am sure, the Lord gave me a special strength, at that moment because He wanted me for Himself alone. Oh, the goodness of God!"[25] Since the Catholic church and the Italian government had outlawed slavery, no authority could remove Bakhita. By the time of her liberation, Bakhita was about twenty years old.

Freedom and the knowledge of the good Lord allowed Bakhita to understand that although she did not know God during slavery, God was still there orchestrating her life and preparing this "lucky one" for himself. Once Bakhita saw the beauty in nature and the kindness of people, she confessed, "Who is the master of these beautiful things?... I had a deep longing to see Him, to know Him, and pay Him homage...."[26] Certainly, in hindsight, we can see that it must have been the hand of God that led Bakhita through slavery and to the Canossians' front door. Her humble way inspired others to seek out the Risen Lord and embrace the gospel as Bakhita did.

The freed Bakhita remained with the sisters and joined the community as a novice in 1893. Almost immediately she learned of the Blessed Virgin Mary's great love for her, saying, "Our Lady protected me, even before I could know Her."[27] On August 10, 1927, she took her final vows as a Canossian sister. Bakhita spent her years in the convent serving mostly as cook, portress and sacristan. No task was too small as all things were done in prayer and for God's glory. During the first and second world wars, Bakhita prayed for the town of Schio where her convent was located. Often the townspeople came to her for comfort and soothing words. The town was spared devastating damage and the people credited Bakhita's prayers for this blessing. As a result, Sister Bakhita, or Mother Moretta (which means "our Black Mother"), as the people called her, was highly regarded throughout the town.

She was also known as the "Universal Sister" because of her love and care for all people regardless of their color. Upon her death in 1947 mothers brought their children to the viewing to place Sister Bakhita's hands upon their children's heads. The children remembered how she entertained them and gave them extra-special love and care, and they loved Mother Moretta back. In this way she could give the children a blessing, for surely she was a saint. Her final words left no doubt of this: "If the Lord allows me to, I'll send many graces from heaven for the salvation of souls."[28]

We must be sure to add that Bakhita's personality of simple compassion and genuine love enabled her to devote herself completely to the gospel and crucified Jesus. It was indeed her personality that permitted the Italian people to love her so dearly. Bakhita's mortal remains rest in a glass urn at the Canossian Convent Chapel in Schio, Italy.

On May 17, 1992, Pope John Paul II beatified Sister Josephine Bakhita. Eight years later on October 1, 2000, Pope John Paul II canonized her Saint Josephine Bakhita in St. Peter's Square.

SCRIPTURE

Then Peter came and said to him, "Lord, if another member of the church sins against me, how often should I forgive? As many as seven times?" Jesus said to him, "Not seven times, but, I tell you, seventy-seven times." (Matthew 18:21–22)

PRAYER

Bakhita, our sister in faith, show us how forgiveness really works! We see how you forgave your captors and embraced the love of Jesus. Daughter of the Sudan, you who emerged out of slavery into the arms of our loving Savior, you continue to guide us with your example and your words. Mother Moretta, you overcame the color barriers and loved everyone so simply, so completely, so bravely. Sister of Charity, you forgave from your heart and God rewarded you as only God could do. Saint Josephine Bakhita, comforter and keeper of the door, pray for us so that we can forgive like you. Amen.

REFLECTION

How do you truly forgive your torturers from your heart? How do you heal your heart and mind so that God can embrace you too?

The Quiet Saint

Saint Benedict the Moor led a very humble and inspiring life in Italy. From his poor beginnings as a slave, Benedict worked on a farm, just like his Christian parents, Christopher and Diana Manasseri, both of whom were slaves. Often these names confuse devotees and cause them to believe that the family was Italian. Benedict's parents actually chose their first names at their baptisms. The last name was that of their owner. Benedict's name offers some level of misunderstanding as well. The term "the Moor" gives false indications that the family was from Morocco or even Portugal. It also suggests that perhaps Benedict was a Muslim at one time. None of this is true. This identifier, *the Moor,* is derived from his childhood since Benedict spent time caring for the sick and performing other acts of service for the poor and helpless. His actions caused people to call him "the black saint" or "the holy black"—"il Moro" in Italian—hence Benedict the Moor.

Though Benedict was never ordained a priest, he accepted the solitary life offered as a lay brother by joining the Order of Friars Minor of the Observance at the Friary of St. Mary of Jesus at Palermo, Italy. As a brother Benedict loved to serve others. He never enjoyed any sort of attention, so he quietly went about his task as a cook. He would have been very content occupying this role for the remainder of his life, but the other monks called upon Benedict to lead them. Reluctantly he accepted the role of guardian and then novice master. After some years he asked to return to the kitchen as the cook. Still, people sought Benedict out for

6

Saint Benedict the Moor
=====
Slave, Monk and Saint

===

1526–1589
Feast Day
April 4

=

advice, miracles and other good works. *Butler's Lives of the Saints* finishes the story well:

> Nevertheless, he was glad when he was released and allowed to return to the kitchen, although his position was scarcely that of the obscure cook of earlier years. Now, all day long, he was beset by visitors of all conditions—the poor demanding alms, the sick seeking to be healed, and distinguished persons requesting his advice or his prayers. Though he never refused to see those who asked for him, he shrank from marks of respect, and when travelling would cover his face with his hood and if possible choose the night that he might not be recognized.[29]

This was the life of Saint Benedict the Moor, the humble servant of God who only wanted to fast, pray and labor for the Lord. His quiet manner and charitable spirit earned him the respect of the clergy and laity of his time.

In 1807 Pope Pius VII canonized Benedict for his holiness and made a public statement against the evils of slavery. This event occurred at the height of the slave trade both in Europe and throughout the Americas. The fact that the Vatican raised up Benedict for this great status in the universal church was a clear sign that holy mother church regarded slavery as an evil against humanity. The significance of Benedict, a freed black slave, now acknowledged for his holiness, cannot be overlooked. Though he is regarded as the patron of African Americans in North America, Benedict's canonization did not hinder or affect the slave trade in North America.

SCRIPTURE

I therefore, the prisoner in the Lord, beg you to lead a life worthy of the calling to which you have been called, with all humility and gentleness, with patience, bearing with one another in love, making every effort to maintain the unity of the Spirit in the bond of peace. (Ephesians 4:1–3)

PRAYER

Dear Saint Benedict, all you desired was solitude and prayer, but you labored for your brothers and others who required your help. In humble service, you performed tasks without complaint. Dear saint of heaven, we ask your assistance as we seek to quietly serve the people of our time. Amen.

REFLECTION

How can you humbly serve in your home, neighborhood and church community?

Saint for Justice

7

Saint Cassian of Tangier

=====

Court Clerk and Martyr

===

d. 298

Feast Day
December 3

=

Cassian of Tangier was not known to be a Christian during his life. In fact, he was a court reporter who became outraged when another Christian was sentenced to death.

In the year 298 Marcellus, a centurion, was being tried for his Christian activities during the persecutions at Tingis, Mauretania (present-day Tangier, Morocco). Although there are some disagreements among hagiographers (those who study the lives of the saints) as to the exact story, it is agreed that Cassian and Marcellus both suffered death at the hands of Roman officials. The most common story gives evidence to Cassian performing his note-taking duties as usual but then throwing down his recording instruments and yelling in the courtroom. His yells were directed toward Aurelius Agricolan, the judge who had just condemned Marcellus to death. Cassian could not remain silent when this injustice had taken place. He was arrested on the spot and beheaded five weeks later after his own trial and conviction for being a Christian. For his actions Saint Cassian is known as a martyr for justice and mercy.

Saint Cassian of Tangier models the ultimate Christian act of brotherhood and friendship. His decision to speak up for what is right clearly left him standing alone in the courtroom and later on at his beheading. There were no groups or persons with him to support his choice. There were no character witnesses to speak up for this one who embraced the unpopular Christian faith. Except for the unconditional love of our redeemer, Cassian was alone. With the simple utterance of "I am a Christian," he was condemned.

One might ask why he didn't remain quiet. In more contemporary times we have witnessed what can happen when men and women remain silent. The transatlantic slave trade, the Holocaust and, more recently, the genocides in Rwanda and Sudan are just a few cases of what happens in our world when silence is the acceptable mode of behavior. Throughout time many good men and women, among them Edmund Burke and Dr. Martin Luther King, Jr., have been quoted as saying, "All that is needed for evil to rise is for men of goodwill to remain silent." I am sure they would agree that our world needs more Saint Cassians.

SCRIPTURE

See, I am sending you out like sheep into the midst of wolves; so be wise as serpents and innocent as doves. Beware of them, for they will hand you over to councils and flog you in their synagogues; and you will be dragged before governors and kings because of me, as a testimony to them and the Gentiles. When they hand you over, do not worry about how you are to speak or what you are to say; for what you are to say will be given to you at that time; for it is not you who speak, but the Spirit of your Father speaking through you. Brother will betray brother to death, and a father his child, and children will rise against parents and have them put to death; and you will be hated by all because of my name. But the one who endures to the end will be saved. When they persecute you in one town, flee to the next; for truly I tell you, you will not have gone through all the towns of Israel before the Son of Man comes. (Matthew 10:16–23)

PRAYER

Saint Cassian, your life was safe! You could have just minded your own business! You could have simply served justice in another way. In speaking out for the wrongly accused and persecuted, you became a martyr for a faith unknown to you. You supported justice for a faith known only to you through official testimony. These Christians were not even your friends. You spoke out for the right. You were standing alone. Now you enjoy the rich company of the saints and eternal glory. Honorable Saint Cassian, help us to speak out for mercy and justice, just like you. When others slander and oppress, we pray for your strength and conviction to stand up and speak out. Amen.

REFLECTION

Why is it so difficult to protect justice in our communities? When crime and violence has taken over neighborhoods, do you assist police and other authorities, or do you remain silent?

Princess Saint

It is my hope that we will begin to hear more about this beautiful religious sister, Theresa Chikaba, who is still not yet well-known. Sister Chikaba was born along the west coast of Africa in an area that is now a part of Guinea. Her father was a king who influenced his children to worship Lucero, the local god of their small kingdom. Chikaba, however, felt disappointment as she witnessed those around her bowing to this god. She wanted more in her spiritual relationship with her creator. The people in her village soon learned that she was gifted in her willingness to always help the less fortunate. Eventually her brothers began to worry that Chikaba would snatch the kingdom from them after their father's death. She assured them that she had other interests.

Spanish sailors kidnapped Chikaba at the age of ten and sold her into slavery. She ended up in Spain serving a nobleman. Fourteen years later, in the year 1700, two significant events happened. First, she was introduced to a prince from her native country. At the request of King Louis XIV of France, Chikaba was offered in marriage to this prince, but she refused. Second, she attempted to enter a convent in Madrid because her true desire was to become a religious sister, but all of them turned her down because of her skin color. After all, who ever heard of a black nun?

Eventually Chikaba was allowed to enter a convent but only as a maid. Once her charity and devotedness to the Virgin Mary and the Blessed Sacrament became known, Theresa Chikaba was fully accepted into the convent of

8

Venerable Theresa
Chikaba
(Theresa Juliana of
Saint Dominic)
=====
Religious

===

1676–1748
Feast Day
December 6

=

the Dominican Sisters of the Third Order of Saint Mary Magdalene. She became Theresa Juliana of Saint Dominic. As a vowed religious, Sister Chikaba was always praying for charity and forgiveness for all. She especially prayed for those who oppressed and hated her because of her color. The people of Salamanca, a city near her convent, believed that Sister Chikaba possessed supernatural powers to heal, prophesy and advise.

After forty-four years in the convent, Sister Chikaba died. Her remains are in the convent of the Dominicans Sisters of Las Duenas in Salamanca. Many miracles have been attributed to Sister Chikaba. Therefore, we should all pray for her canonization.

SCRIPTURE

Now the eleven disciples went to Galilee, to the mountain to which Jesus had directed them. When they saw him, they worshiped him; but some doubted. And Jesus came and said to them, "All authority in heaven and on earth has been given to me. Go therefore and make disciples of all nations, baptizing them in the name of the Father and of the Son and of the Holy Spirit, and teaching them to obey everything that I have commanded you. And remember, I am with you always, to the end of the age." (Matthew 28:16–20)

PRAYER

Dear Sister Chikaba, your prayers are priceless! Certainly your life presented countless hardships, but you answered every adversity with prayer. How did you manage to turn the evil wished upon you into prayers of penance? When those around you hated and scorned you, you prayed. You prayed when you were denied comfort and human dignity, but you continued to pray even more for the unfaithful. Most gracious Chikaba, you remained devoted to the Blessed Sacrament and the Blessed Virgin Mary. Please pray for us, that we can remain faithful, too, especially during our weary and tearful moments here on earth. Amen.

REFLECTION

How do you remain faithful when life presents challenges to you? When you lose a job, a family member dies or other tragedies occur, what steps do you take to remain faithful?

Saint of Unity

Saint Cyprian, a model of unity and forgiveness in our church, began his life of service as a pagan lawyer and teacher. After his conversion to Christianity he became known for his theological teachings, church leadership and spirit of unity. He was immediately devoted to the church and readily spoke out against the heretical teachings of his day.

His devotion caused Cyprian to go into hiding during the persecutions of Emperor Decius (r. 250–251). According to the *New Catholic Encyclopedia,* he continued "directing and encouraging his clergy and faithful from his place of hiding and resisting the insubordination of some of the priests and of the confessors who were pandering to the lapsed."[30] It must have taken great inner strength to offer such guidance through messages and letters only, especially when the priests under his leadership were ignoring his requests. When Cyprian returned to Carthage (in present-day Tunisia), he insisted that penances were required for the Christians who sacrificed to pagan gods during the time of persecution.

Still plagued by divisions within the church, Cyprian spoke out against the Novatianists, those who wanted the lapsi (those Christians who sacrificed to pagan gods) to return to the church without doing any form of penance. His arguments against Novatian and his followers were crucial as the controversy was causing severe division within the church. Further, Cyprian felt that all baptisms administered by the Novatianists must be redone as they were performed outside of the confines of

9

Saint Cyprian of
Carthage
=====
Father of the Church,
Bishop and Martyr

===

ca. 200–258
Feast Day
September 16

=

church authority and therefore invalid. In his view, all sacraments had to be sanctioned by the church to be of value or else church unity was in jeopardy.

The argument lingered until Pope Stephen ruled that no Christian could be rebaptized. Cyprian refused to relent to the pope and bad blood settled between them, even when Stephen threatened to excommunicate Cyprian for not obeying orders from Rome. The issue died down as Emperor Valerian issued his new persecution orders in the year 257. The first of Valerian's orders required all bishops, priests and deacons to make sacrifices to the Roman gods. When Cyprian refused, he was arrested and exiled to the town of Curubis. Valerian later ordered that all bishops, priests and deacons be executed. Although he had an opportunity to escape (the proconsul ordered Cyprian to Utica, but he ignored the order), Cyprian preferred to accept martyrdom for his people without any argument or debate with authorities. He believed that his martyrdom would speak louder than words. Cyprian, bishop of Carthage, was beheaded surrounded by his parishioners and deacons. In the book *Martyrs* author Donald Attwater describes the situation:

> Cyprian was taken to the field of Sextus, where people climbed trees to get a better view. He took off his cloak and knelt down, bowing in prayer to the Lord. Then he took off his tunic, handing it to his deacons and stood up in his linen undergarment to wait for the executioner; on his arrival Cyprian directed that twenty-five gold coins be given him. The brethren spread linen cloths on the ground around their bishop, and he blindfolded himself, but could not tie the ends of the handkerchief and a priest and a subdeacon, both named Julian, did it for him. Thus did blessed Cyprian suffer.[31]

We know so much about Saint Cyprian because of his courage in addressing every heresy of his time. He also took the time to address specific pastoral and social issues that affected the people in his care. His letters, which include a defense of Christianity against paganism, an exhortation to those expecting martyrdom, a commentary on the Our Father, a conference for consecrated virgins, and reflections on charity and jealousy, gave his people some guidance in turbulent times.

Through his eighty-one known letters, Cyprian shows his strength of character, his devotion to the church and love for the people of Carthage. No threats against his mortal life would deter Saint Cyprian from this resolve.

SCRIPTURE

Blessed are those who hunger and thirst for righteousness, for they will be filled. (Matthew 5:6)

PRAYER

Saint Cyprian, in the spirit of unity and hope, you called together the church of your time to truly forgive just as Jesus did. You modeled the unconditional love ever-present through the Risen Lord who loves and forgives us and will do so until the end of time. With your fine example of Christian compassion, we clearly see our duties as disciples of our time. Saint Cyprian, help us to be more forgiving, just like you. Amen.

REFLECTION

In what ways can you help create unity in your home, community or parish? How can you properly and effectively address issues that need attention within your community?

The Energetic Saint

Saint Gelasius was certainly a busy pope. At the time of his papacy he was second only to Leo I in terms of his papal activities. Additionally, Gelasius inherited the Acacian schism as he ascended the papacy in the year 492. This split involved the patriarch Acacius of Constatinople who appointed Monophysite bishops (believing that Christ's humanity was swallowed up by his divinity). These new bishops did not support the Catholic doctrine that Jesus was fully human and fully divine.

The bishops' appointments were unacceptable to Gelasius. He continued to argue this issue even after Acacius died, at which time Gelasius insisted that Acacius's name be erased from the public records of the respected dead. Gelasius's insistence and the new patriarch's refusal ushered in a new debate for this pope. He was now faced with a disagreement between church and state.

Among the other issues, Gelasius argued for papal infallibility. He advocated divine authority for the papacy. He also fought against Pelagianism (a belief system that denied original sin and humanity's inclination to do evil, advocated that each person is able to obtain his or her own moral good and that no one needs God's grace) and Manichaeanism (which advocated the church of the mind where human beings can change the aspects of good versus evil). His efforts against the latter caused church leaders to accept his insistence that people must receive the Eucharist in two species so as to contradict the Manicheans, who said that wine was impure and preached against drinking it.

IO

Pope Saint Gelasius I

=====

The Forty-Ninth Pope

===

r. 492–496

Feast Day
November 21

=

Although Gelasius was quite busy fighting, he amazingly found adequate time to write over one hundred letters and treatises. Most of these survive today. There is also a Sacramentary that bears his name, but it is doubtful that he actually wrote it. It is more probable that his teachings influenced it in some way and thus the Sacramentary was attributed to him.

Pope Saint Gelasius can be seen as a strict, unyielding pope bent on protecting the faith. He can also be described as a humble, unselfish servant fully prepared to respond to the needs of his people. History reveals that Gelasius was wealthy at one time, but he gave his riches to the poor, thus exposing his nature as a humble servant to God's people.

We know that Gelasius was the first pope referred to as the "Vicar of Christ." From our knowledge of this great pope, the title is very applicable due to his strength of will, devotion to doctrine and love of the people. Pope Saint Gelasius was buried in St. Peter's Basilica after serving the church very energetically and prayerfully.

SCRIPTURE

Now when Jesus heard that John had been arrested, he withdrew to Galilee. He left Nazareth and made his home in Capernaum by the lake, in the territory of Zebulun and Naphtali, so that what had been spoken through the prophet Isaiah might be fulfilled:

"Land of Zebuln, land of Naphtali,
    on the road by the sea, across the Jordan, Galilee of the
        Gentiles—
the people who sat in darkness
    have seen a great light,
and for those who sat in the region and shadow of death
    light has dawned."

From that time Jesus began to proclaim, "Repent, for the kingdom of heaven has come near."

As he walked by the Sea of Galilee, he saw two brothers, Simon, who is called Peter, and Andrew his brother, casting a net into the sea—for they were fishermen. And he said to them, "Follow me, and I will make you fish for people." Immediately they left their nets and followed him. As he went from there, he saw two other brothers,

James son of Zebedee and his brother John, in the boat with their father Zebedee, mending their nets, and he called them. Immediately they left the boat with their father, and followed him. (Matthew 4:12–22)

PRAYER

Dear Pope Saint Gelasius, you were quite busy! Your model of leadership is an inspiration to every leader. Help us to be devoted to the church like you. Amen.

REFLECTION

How can you become a leader in your church? How can you support the leaders already in active church ministry?

The Martyred Slave

Historians do not know a lot about Saint Julia of Carthage (sometimes her name appears as Saint Julia of Carthage and Corsica), but what is known reveals the strength and conviction of a martyr. Her story takes place in Carthage in North Africa (in present-day Tunisia). In 439 a tribe known as the Vandals invaded Carthage and began their barbaric reign over Europe and parts of Africa. Julia was sold as a slave by the Vandals. Her owner was a Syrian merchant named Eusebius who respected Julia and her Christian faith. When Eusebius sailed to Corsica, he took Julia with him but did not allow her to leave the ship. The governor in Corsica insisted that Eusebius bring Julia to the pagan festival but he refused, knowing that she would not participate in the pagan festivities. That night after Eusebius had fallen asleep, the governor had Julia brought ashore, but she refused to participate in their sacrifices. The governor ordered her execution at once. She was promptly crucified before Eusebius woke from his drink-induced sleep.

This is all we know about Saint Julia of Carthage. The information seems brief, but the impact of her life is significant as the church considers her martyrdom important. Her humility and strength in enslavement caused her owner to respect her as well as her faith.

SCRIPTURE

He has told you, O mortal, what is good;
    and what does the LORD require of you

II

Saint Julia of Carthage
=====
Slave and Martyr

===

Fifth Century
Feast Day
May 22

=

but to do justice, and to love kindness,
    and to walk humbly with your God? (Micah 6:8)

PRAYER

Saint Julia, your owner respected your faith but you were martyred by the hands of another authority. As a martyr of your time, you refused freedom and accepted death, even death on the cross. How did you do this? If only you performed one pagan sacrifice, freedom from slavery and a new life would have been yours, but you refused. Making such a choice must have been hard—or was it easier because of your faith? Dear Saint Julia, we face no forms of imposed slavery or torture but still look to you as a Christian witness who made a clear choice about the faith. Help us to make clear choices too, especially when we are alone, frightened or oppressed. Amen.

REFLECTION

Do you treat the faith like a smorgasbord dinner, selecting what's acceptable for you at the time? Or do you accept the full embodiment of what the church requires of you? How do you walk humbly with your God?

The Evangelization Saints

The story of Saint Charles Lwanga and the Ugandan Martyrs reaches out to us today with shock and horror, yet wonder and awe. It is truly difficult for us to imagine how young people could shoulder the experience of martyrdom so courageously. Charles Lwanga and companions, while still in their teens and twenties, embraced Christianity when it was dangerous in their country's history.

Their story begins in 1879 when King Mutesa of the Bugandan kingdom of Uganda accepted Christianity into the country. After his death the next king, Mwanga, began a policy of exterminating Christians, both Catholics and Protestants. The new king took Joseph Musaka Balikuddembe as his chief steward. Joseph, a Christian, took every opportunity to speak out against the king's behavior with the young page boys at the palace. These confrontations did not go well with King Mwanga, especially after Joseph spoke out against the murder of an Anglican missionary. Joseph was the first Ugandan martyr killed because he professed to be a Christian and refused to remain silent about King Mwanga's activities.

Charles Lwanga took Joseph's place at the palace. He did everything in his power to protect the young pages, but King Mwanga quickly became aware that the boys were receiving instruction on becoming Christians. Immediately, King Mwanga ordered all Christians to be rounded up. Charles Lwanga led everyone in prayer as he baptized the page boys himself. Eventually they were caught and placed before the king, who demanded to know who

12

Saint Charles Lwanga
and Companions
=====
Youth Leaders and Martyrs

===

1865–1886
Feast Day
June 3

=

was a Christian. He ordered the young men, "Those of you who do not pray, stand by me. Those who pray [those who are Christians], go over there." The king spoke to the group of Christians, "Then you shall all be burnt! Away with you, and you can eat cow in Heaven!"[32]

The king ordered Charles and the boys to be burned alive. It is important to note that there were other martyrs—at least twenty-three Protestant young men. The Catholic martyrs are listed below.

Charles Lwanga, age 25
Matthias Kalemba, age 50
Joseph Mukasa Balikuddembe, age 25
Denis Ssebuggwawo, age 16
Pontian Ngondwe, age 35
Andrew Kaggwa, age 30
Athanasius Bazzeketta, age 20
Gonzaga Gonza, age 24
Noe Mwahhali, age 35
Luke Banabakintu, age 30
James Buzabaliawo, age 25
Gyavira, age 17
Ambrose Kibuka, age 18
Anatole Kiriggwajjo, age 20
Achilles Kiwanuka, age 17
Kizito, age 14
Mbaga Tuzinde, age 17
Mugagga, age 16
Mukasa Kiriwawanvu, age 20
Dolphus Mukasa Ludigo, age 24
Bruno Serunkuma, age 30
Jean-Marie Muzeyi, age 30

The sacrifice of these young martyrs was recognized on October 18, 1964, as Pope Paul VI raised them all to sainthood. This pope of modern times signaled the rise of the Catholic church in Africa with the pronouncement that:

> ...We add to the glorious list of saints triumphant in heaven these twenty-two sons of Africa....

Who are they? They are Africans first of all. By their colour, race and culture they are true Africans descended from the Bantu race and the peoples of the Upper Nile....

Yes, they are Africans and they are martyrs....

[T]he injustice and violence which led to it tend to fade from human memory, while before the eyes of succeeding generations there remains ever present the shining example of a meekness which has transformed the laying down of life.... Such is the true meaning of martyrdom.[33]

SCRIPTURE

For all who are led by the Spirit of God are children of God. For you did not receive a spirit of slavery to fall back into fear, but you have received a spirit of adoption. When we cry, "Abba! Father!" it is that very Spirit bearing witness with our spirit that we are children of God, and if children, then heirs, heirs of God and joint heirs with Christ—if, in fact, we suffer with him so that we may also be glorified with him. (Romans 8:14–17)

PRAYER

Saint Charles Lwanga, wow! How strong and brave of you to practice Christianity knowing the danger around you. You were young but possessed the wisdom of ages. All throughout your ordeal, you maintained your focus on the Risen Lord. *Bravery? Maturity? Strength?* What are the proper words to describe your resolve? Your actions showed us that you are a true child of God. Help us, especially when faced with difficulties, to know that we are children of God and joint heirs with Christ and you. Amen.

REFLECTION

How do you proclaim that you are a child of God and joint heir with Christ? In your lowest moments of despair, can you still show and proclaim this?

The Humble Saint

13

Saint Martin de Porres

=====

Lay Brother and Visionary

===

1579–1639

Feast Day
November 3

=

A gentle, loving and happy demeanor is characteristic of Martin de Porres of Lima, Peru. From his poor beginnings as the son of Juan de Porres, a Spanish nobleman who abandoned the family, and Ana Velazquez, a freed slave, Martin was always a gentle soul. There are two possible reasons his father abandoned the family: His son looked African and did not have the lighter complexion that Juan expected; or because it was still illegal in Spain to marry Africans. Since Juan de Porres worked for the king, he probably believed it best for himself that he leave the family in order to secure his job. Once the money that he left for the care of Martin, his mother and sister, Juana, ran out, Ana set out to find work and young Martin had to help his struggling family.

Sometimes Martin was not so helpful as he had the habit of giving his family's meager food and funds away to anyone who seemed to be worse off. His heart could not let anyone or anything suffer if he had the power to help. Martin endured his mother's anger and punishments, as often his own family had nothing to eat. But this did not last for long as Juan de Porres returned to claim his children en route to Ecuador to assume his new position as governor. In Ecuador Juana and Martin received an education and had plenty to eat.

When Martin turned twelve, his father arranged an apprenticeship for him as a barber-surgeon. This was a great opportunity for Martin to use his skills to help those in need. In this new trade Martin could cut hair, nurse the sick and give out medicine. He remained in his apprenticeship for approximately three years before he petitioned the Dominican Order to accept him as a "simple servant." (Sources vary as to his exact status within the Dominicans.)[34] Though his father wanted Martin to become a brother, Martin refused since he wanted only to serve others.

Martin was accepted into the Dominican Order and assigned to sweep the monastery. He was also assigned the jobs that no one wanted, like cleaning the toilets and washing dishes. Of course, Martin performed his duties with a smile, always thanking the good Lord for the chance to serve. Because he was a trained barber, Martin was also assigned to cut the brothers' hair and work with the sick. This he did prayerfully and without complaint. Even when the brothers did not appreciate Martin's contributions and resorted to rebuking him and calling him names, Martin would only reply, "You have only spoken the truth. Please forgive this miserable sinner."[35]

In addition to his other duties, Martin served the community as the gardener, cook and helper to the poor. He always made a special effort to feed those in need. There is a story of Martin feeding the crowds of Peru: One day Brother Sebastian was portioning out servings and realized that there was not enough for the poor. Brother Martin came to help and said, "There's no need to worry…. Doesn't God provide for the flowers of the field? He'll take care of us as well." There was barely enough soup for six people but Martin served everyone in the crowd. He even had enough for the dogs and cats.[36]

This great saint serves as a model for our time. He provided an example of friendship, humility and service to a world that did not always appreciate his gifts. Martin de Porres's pleasant manner and dedication to duty can assist us, even in our twenty-first–century world.

It is also fascinating to note Martin's special abilities, which were observed in the monastery. The brothers reported numerous miracles, healings and Martin's special ability to bilocate and levitate. These astounding stories include one in which a visitor to the monastery recognized Martin from when he appeared to him as a prisoner in Algeria. The other brothers were amazed because Martin had never traveled outside of Peru.

Even the animals listened to Martin. Once an angry bull was running through the monastery. Martin talked to the bull saying,

"Brother Bull, you are causing havoc here. Return to the street where you belong."[37] At these words, the bull departed. Another account has Martin instructing mice to stop eating holes in the altar cloths. They, too, obeyed his request since Martin spoke out of love for the mice as well as all animals.

After a life of fasting, poverty and extreme mortification, Martin de Porres died at the age of sixty with his brothers around him lovingly chanting the *Salve Regina*. He continued to perform miracles immediately after his death for the brothers and the people of Peru. At his funeral so many mourners tore off parts of his habit for relics that his habit had to be changed several times. It was reported that a sweet odor emanated from his body throughout his burial services. Some regarded this as the "odor of sanctity."

During his life Martin de Porres healed the sick, comforted the dying, fed the poor and housed the orphans, all the while remaining joyful that God provides for and blesses God's people. For his holiness and devotion to others, he was declared venerable in 1763, beatified in 1837 and canonized in 1962.

SCRIPTURE

Blessed are the meek, for they will inherit the earth.
Blessed are those who hunger and thirst for righteousness, for they
will be filled.
Blessed are the merciful, for they will receive mercy.
Blessed are the pure in heart, for they will see God.
Blessed are the peacemakers, for they will be called children of God.
Blessed are those who are persecuted for righteousness' sake, for theirs
is the kingdom of heaven. (Matthew 5:5–10)

PRAYER

Good and humble Saint Martin de Porres, we need your help! How could you take on the most menial of jobs? It seemed that you loved the tasks that no one else desired. Always you decreased yourself, but God, in God's wonderful wisdom, increased your gifts. God blessed you with so many spiritual abilities that others flocked to you with the hope of a blessing. Thank you for your example of humility and quiet service to others. We pray that we can do likewise for our neighbors and friends. Amen.

REFLECTION

How do you react when hateful words and actions are thrown your way? What steps can you take to be a spiritual and physical servant to others? How can you be careful not to boast about your every achievement and blessing?

14

Saint Mary of Egypt
=====
Prostitute and Hermit

===

Fifth Century
Feast Day
April 2

=

The Hermit Saint

Fact or fiction? Which applies to the historical reality about Saint Mary of Egypt? Did she really live in the fifth century as a prostitute (some accounts say she was a singer and dancer) who turned into a hermit? Or was she merely a popular myth generated by tales of oral tradition? Whatever the truth, there are two accounts of her life, neither of which became popular until two hundred years after her death.

Both accounts reveal that Mary ran away from home at the age of twelve. We do not know if she was forced but we do know that her parents were still alive when she departed. She then fell into a life of prostitution. Mary remained in this state, according to Robert Fulton Holtzclaw in *The Saints Go Marching In,* "for seventeen years, not for money, but because she enjoyed it."[38]

Mary then set off to the Holy Land to practice her trade there, but her life began to change. She attempted to enter the Church of the Holy Sepulchre but was thrown back by some mysterious force, as she was an unrepentant sinner. When she came to this realization, she prayed to the Blessed Mother asking for guidance to sin no more. After this prayer Mary entered the church and began a life of repentance as a hermit. This is where the two accounts of her life part.

One account describes Mary wandering in the desert near the Jordan River. Two disciples of Saint Cyriacus encountered her to hear the story of her life. She explained that she was in the desert to repent for her many sinful years. On hearing this they returned to Cyriacus and the three men set out to see Mary but found her dead.

Another account of this repentant hermit is more glorious and merits more discussion. It details the journey of a monk named Zozimus who left his monastery to wander the Jordan River and desert area. He encountered Mary who told her tale of sin and repentance in the desert. Zozimus promised to return the next year and give Mary Communion, which he did. As he saw her across the river, she reportedly walked on water to meet him as Zozimus stood on the other side. The surprised monk offered Mary food but she would only accept three lentils. When Zozimus returned the following year, he found Mary dead at their meeting place.

Her story merits discussion as this holy woman repented not only for her sins but for the sins of the world. As she endured great hardship with lack of food (she ate only herbs and dates), mortification and abuses caused by the ever-changing desert weather, Mary continued to pray.

SCRIPTURE

Jesus said to her, "Go, call your husband, and come back." The woman answered him, "I have no husband." Jesus said to her, "You are right in saying, 'I have no husband'; for you have had five husbands, and the one you have now is not your husband. What you have said is true!" The woman said to him, "Sir, I see that you are a prophet." (John 4:16–19)

PRAYER

Mary, wow! See how God forgives all. The story of your life gives hope to those of us living in a sinful existence. You were so young to be on your own but you managed to survive with God's loving hands waiting for you. In your life of seclusion you must have heard the sweet voice of Jesus many times echoing through the desert calm. Dearest Mary, show us how to hear the Lord in the golden silence and calm moments of our lives. Help us to turn our lives around as well. Amen.

REFLECTION

When you are alone, one-on-one with the Lord, how do you hear his sweet voice? Should you develop a spiritual exercise to truly hear when God is trying to tell you something?

The Soldier Saints

15

Saint Maurice and the
Theban Legion
=====
Soldiers and Martyrs

===

d. 287
Feast Day
September 22

=

One brave Egyptian general who served in the Roman army received orders from his emperor, Diocletian, to take 6,600 men to Gaul (present-day France) to quash a rebellion against Emperor Maximian, who was persecuting Christians. This general's name was Maurice and unknown to both of those emperors, Maurice and his men (known as the Theban Legion) were Christians themselves. Maurice marched his men to Gaul and encountered the enemy near Lake Geneva (in present-day Switzerland). There he discovered that the Gauls were Christians, too. Immediately, he sent word to Maximian that he could not fight the Christians because he too was a Christian. When Maximian arrived at Lake Geneva, at a place called Aganaum, he ordered Maurice and his legion to make a sacrifice to the Roman gods. Maurice and two of his officers, Candidus and Exuperius, refused on behalf of the legion. They appealed to the emperor in this way:

> We are your soldiers, but are also the servants of the true God. We owe you military service and obedience; but we cannot renounce Him who is our Creator and Master.... We have taken an oath to God before we took one to you: you can place no confidence in our second oath if we violate the first.[39]

Emperor Maximian turned his attention to the legion and ordered them to perform the sacrifice. With their refusal, he ordered every tenth man executed. Still the legion and their general, Maurice, remained steadfast. Every tenth man was executed again until the entire legion was slaughtered.

While some historians wish to debate the historical accuracy of the slaughter, no one debates that Maurice was, in fact, martyred. His remains were discovered and identified by Saint Theodore, bishop of Octudurm, in 350. Saint Theodore built a basilica at Aganaum (present-day Saint Maurice en Valais or Saint-Moritz) and enshrined the relics there. Robert Fulton Holtzclaw in *The Saints Go Marching In* offers these asides to the story of Saint Maurice: "Unlike many of the other saints, no miracles are attributed to St. Maurice and his army. He is now the principal saint of Southern Germany, parts of France, Switzerland, Spain and Italy.... He is the patron saint of dyers, weavers and swordsmiths. Sufferers from the gout pray to him for his intercession. The Sardinain [*sic*] Order of St. Maurice, the highest civilian medal in Italy, is named for him."[40]

SCRIPTURE

Then the people answered, "Far be it from us that we should forsake the LORD to serve other gods; for it is the LORD our God who brought us and our ancestors up from the land of Egypt, out of the house of slavery, and who did those great signs in our sight. He protected us along all the way that we went, and among all the peoples through whom we passed; and the LORD drove out before us all the peoples, the Amorites who lived in the land. Therefore we also will serve the LORD, for he is our God." (Joshua 24:16–18)

PRAYER

Brave Saint Maurice, you were determined to be a Christian. No threats leveled against you would distract you from the love of the Lord. Though your legion numbered in the thousands, their faithfulness prevailed over the emperor's threats. Saint Maurice, through your bravery, you teach us that taking a stand for what you believe in is always right. As a leader, your courage inspired men to do the same, all in the name of Jesus, our redeemer. Amen.

REFLECTION

How can you take a stand to show that you are a Christian? As a leader, you may be called on publicly to say, "but as for me and my household, we will serve the LORD" (Joshua 24:15). How can you say this in twenty-first–century circumstances?

Pope for Peace

Pope Miltiades (also known as Melchiades) served as pope during a time of peace that followed Emperor Constantine's end to the persecution of Christians in the Roman Empire. How significant for Miltiades, an African pope, to occupy the papacy at this time. One of the problems he did have to deal with, however, was the split caused by the Donatists (led by Donatus, who taught that sacraments performed by lapsed priests needed to be redone). This split proved to be a major issue in the African church due to charges leveled against Caecilian, the new bishop of Carthage (in present-day Tunisia).

The Donatists, convinced they were right, intensely argued for new sacraments. Their positions caused quite the stir, as now the church needed to address whether grace, once issued, can be taken back. The Donatists believed that grace was never given, since sinful priests made the sacraments invalid. It was as if the sacraments never took place—all empty gestures, as far as they were concerned.

Miltiades answered this dilemma by ruling that all sacraments were valid and could not be redone and that the worthiness of a priest was not an issue. In the twenty-first century if we were to ask, "Can a person be rebaptized?" the answer would be, "Of course not!" Our creed states that we believe in one baptism for the forgiveness of sins.

In the heat of Miltiades' decree and the Donatists' protests, Emperor Constantine asked for a commission to settle the matter. Miltiades used the commission to stack the deck against

Pope Saint Miltiades

=====

The Thirty-Second Pope

===

r. ca. 311–314

Feast Day
December 10

=

the Donatists. He added fifteen more bishops to the commission and convened a church synod. Of course this was more than Constantine requested, but Miltiades moved ahead with the synod. In the end Donatus was excommunicated, and Miltiades's position was accepted.

Quite fascinating was the emperor's decision to convene a council at Arles to address the matter again. More fascinating was that Miltiades never became upset over the emperor's failure to recognize his ruling as final. The matter subsided when Miltiades died in 314, but the Donatists continued to advocate their position until the Vandals, an eastern Germanic tribe, invaded in the year 439.

Miltiades was buried in the catacombs on the Appian Way, an ancient Roman road, and later moved to St. Peter's Basilica.

SCRIPTURE

When it was evening on that day, the first day of the week, and the doors of the house where the disciples had met were locked for fear of the Jews, Jesus came and stood among them and said, "Peace be with you." After he said this, he showed them his hands and his side. Then the disciples rejoiced when they saw the Lord. Jesus said to them again, "Peace be with you. As the Father has sent me, so I send you." When he had said this, he breathed on them and said to them, "Receive the Holy Spirit. If you forgive the sins of any, they are forgiven them; if you retain the sins of any, they are retained." (John 20:19–23)

PRAYER

Dear Pope Miltiades, we pray that all will one day know of your marvelous deeds as pope. You remained steadfast against the heretics of your day and ushered your people into a time of peace. How refreshing to know of your achievement, especially when our church does not promote your African identity and role within the church. We pray for more church leaders of African decent who are willing to accept the role of servant to us all. Amen.

REFLECTION

How are you recognizing church leaders of today? Do you support their leadership and sacrifice? What steps are you taking to prepare yourself and your children for leadership within the church?

The Counselor Saint

Saint Monica of Tagaste, Numidia (part of Algeria today), serves in our church as the patron saint of wives and mothers. Through her example of motherly love and wifely patience and wisdom, she models for the universal church a life of unconditional love filled with virtuous piety.

Monica was born into a prominent Catholic family. Her youth was centered around her family and her faith. Being raised so close to the city of Carthage (the site of countless acts of martyrdom in present-day Tunisia), Monica was well aware of many acts of courage, especially in the examples of Saints Felicitas and Perpetua in the year 203. Surely she was attuned to the anti-Christian sentiment and acts of persecution that filled the continent. It was in this tradition of courage and survival that Monica was formed as a young woman of her time.

Even as a child, Monica knew and embraced the Gospels. She understood the strict lessons imposed by her maidservant as she was ever obedient even when chastised. Her son Saint Augustine related numerous stories of his mother's youth in North Africa. Both the virtuous and the vain are recorded in his *Confessions*, which speaks of his mother developing a vice:

> By custom her parents used to send her, a sober girl, to fetch wine from the cask. She would plunge the cup through the aperture at the top. Before she poured the wine into a jug, she used to take a tiny sip with the tip of her lips. She could not take more as she disliked the taste. What led her to do this was not an appetite for liquor but the surplus high spirits of a younger person, which

17

Saint Monica
=====
Wife and Mother

===

331–387
Feast Day
August 28

=

can overflow in playful impulses and which in children adults ordinarily try to suppress. Accordingly, to that sip of wine she added more sips every day...until she had fallen into the habit of gulping down almost full cups of wine.[41]

Monica continued with this habit and was caught partaking of the wine by her slave. This maid reproached her mistress by calling her "a bibber of pure wine, a drunkard...an alcoholic."[42]

As a pious and obedient young woman, Monica accepted the correction immediately and gave up the habit of drinking. Her understanding nature early in life foreshadowed her unceasing correction of Augustine, who too often imbibed life's ills. Monica's early life definitely prepared her for her later years, which were filled with grief and uncertainty.

When Monica approached the age of marriage, her father arranged a union with a pagan landowner named Patricius. This union presented some positive as well as some negative aspects for Monica. On the surface there were positive points: Patricius could afford to maintain the lifestyle to which Monica was accustomed. He held status in the community as a landowner. Most importantly, Monica's father regarded Patricius as a good match for his daughter. But the negative points, including the fact that Patricius did not understand the call of Christianity and that he was unfaithful, abusive and ignorant to the demands of the Christian lifestyle, outweighed the positive. Frequently, Patricius would find things for Monica to do just at the time for worship, or he would demand her attention just when she attempted to visit the sick or assist others in need.

How did Monica survive living with such a pagan mate? She always prayed and presented herself as a virtuous woman. According to Leon Cristiani in *Monica and Her Son Augustine,* "Her favorite weapon was patience. She said nothing."[43] "She knew, she saw, but she kept quiet and suffered in silence. She prayed, and probably wept, but she realized that the religion of the pagans condoned great moral degradation.... In her heart, she contrasted the demands of the Christian faith with the laxity of the pagans. She waited for her husband's heart to be won to faith...."[44]

Throughout her long years of prayer, she remained ever-faithful and obedient to her husband and finally witnessed his conversion on his deathbed. Such were her constant years of fulfilling her duty as wife to the unfaithful and often violent Patricius that the other women in her town sought her counsel. They, too, suffered at the hands of violent husbands and desired some peace within their marriages, the peace that they observed in Monica. Of course, she instructed these women to pray and to remain faithful to their husbands, their families and to the Gospels.

Monica's heartbreak did not end with her unfaithful, pagan husband. From her story we know that she gave birth to three children: two boys, Augustine and Navigius, and one girl, Perpetua, named after the great martyr of Carthage.

Both Navigius and Perpetua led Christian lives. Navigius helped his mother a great deal as she lamented over the conduct of her older son, Augustine. Navigius was very different from Augustine and, according to Cristiani, "a fine man, devout, gentle, intelligent, well-educated, but also timid, retiring, silent and apparently of frail health."[45] Perpetua was married, but was later widowed and eventually became a nun. In some Christian documents these two offspring of Monica are listed as blesseds. To Saint Monica's credit, all three of her children are revered in the annals of the Catholic church.

The story of Augustine, Monica's oldest child, is told in an earlier chapter. But, it is important to remember his early life of wandering from heresy to heresy, his affair with a woman that produced a son outside the bonds of marriage and his refusal to embrace the true faith as presented in the Gospels. These actions of Augustine caused great anguish for his mother. Such was her grief that she daily prayed and followed Augustine around from city to city. She prayed that Augustine would abandon his ways and sometimes even harassed her son about how he lived. She remained steadfast with her insistence that Augustine become a Christian. To her great delight, he was baptized in 387 at Milan during the Easter Vigil.

The same year of her son's baptism, Monica wished to depart this life, as she shared with her Augustine:

> My son, as for myself, I now find no pleasure in this life. What I have still to do here and why I am here, I do not

know. My hope in this world is already fulfilled. The one reason why I wanted to stay longer in this life was my desire to see you a Catholic Christian before I die. My God has granted this in a way more than I had hoped. For I see you despising this world's success to become his servant. What have I to do here?[46]

Within a week of her words, Monica returned home to God. The moment that she died those in attendance wept and prayed, except her son, Augustine, who wrote in his *Confessions:* "I closed her eyes and an overwhelming grief welled into my heart and was about to flow forth in floods of tears. But at the same time under a powerful act of mental control my eyes held back the flood and dried it up."[47]

Augustine would eventually weep for this great woman who loved him unceasingly. Only a day after Monica's burial, he shed tears that seemed never to end.

Now I let flow the tears which I had held back so that they ran as freely as they wished. My heart rested upon them, and it reclined upon them because it was your ears that were there, not those of some human critic who would put a proud interpretation on my weeping.... I wept for my mother...who had died before my eyes who had wept for me that I might live before your eyes....[48]

Saint Monica, wife, mother, counselor, Catholic woman, servant of God and professor of the gospel, influenced her family and community in priceless ways. Her devout attention to her wayward son leaves with us a saintly mark on the history of the church in such a way that hope and faithfulness become the realities for all who believe in the Risen Christ. When we consider the role models of the Catholic church, Saint Monica must indeed enter the conversation.

SCRIPTURE

Rejoice always, pray without ceasing, give thanks in all circumstances; for this is the will of God in Christ Jesus for you. Do not quench the Spirit. Do not despise the words of prophets, but test everything; hold fast to what is good; abstain from every form of evil. (1 Thessalonians 5:16–22)

PRAYER

Dear Monica, mother figure for all mothers, the wives and mothers of our time seek your aid. As you counseled the women of your time, please continue to advise all mothers. Our children wander from place to place, from idea to idea, seeking meaning and truth for their existence just as Augustine, your son, did. You know our pain, our prayers and desires for them. You, who endured abuse, neglect and downheartedness, come to our aid. Show us the way to peace and faithfulness, the only way that can lead to our Savior's embrace. Amen.

REFLECTION

How can Monica's example of faith inspire you? What spiritual qualities do you possess to assist you on this journey of faith? How can you "pray without ceasing" (1 Thessalonians 5:17) amid confusion, disappointments and emotional crises?

The Outlaw Saint

The life of Moses the Black allows the faithful to witness God's love and forgiveness for all men and women who search for a clean heart dedicated to the service of others. Truly this was a life turned around from evil to good, by the redeeming love of a marvelous Savior.

Moses was born around 330 in Egypt where he eventually worked as a servant to a wealthy Egyptian family. But his duties and employment were terminated because of his constant stealing. When Moses found himself homeless and without work, he turned to a life of crime and violence, so appalling that his conversion must have been deep. The fact that Moses the villainous criminal could become Saint Moses the much loved and respected Abba, martyr and saint offers hope to the world that a saintly life is always possible.

Moses' exploits are shocking and overwhelming. We know that he robbed, assaulted and murdered people often without cause. Once when a barking dog foiled an attempted robbery, Moses set off to kill the dog owner in retaliation. *Butler's Lives of the Saints* tells the story:

> Once some contemplated villainy was spoiled by the barking of a sheep-dog giving the alarm, and Moses swore to kill the shepherd. To get at him he had to swim across the Nile with his sword in his teeth, but the shepherd had hidden himself by burrowing into the sand; Moses could not find him, so he made up for it by killing four rams, tying them together and towing them back across the river. Then he flayed

18

Saint Moses the Black

=====

Villain and Holy Monk

===

330–405
Feast Day
August 28

=

the rams, cooked and ate the best parts, sold the skins for wine, and walked fifty miles to join his fellows.[49]

Although we know a lot about his life of crime, Moses' conversion experience remains somewhat of a mystery. One story claims that he observed some monks in the desert of Skete and admired their peace and kindness. In this light he turned his life away from villainy and embraced a life devoted to prayer, peace and brotherhood. The desert afforded Moses the opportunity to practice the virtues instead of the vices.

Eventually Moses was ordained by the Bishop of Alexandria, Theophilus. He lived the remaining years of his life at the monastery of Skete as a monk, exuding love and peace toward all men and women. During this time as a monk, Moses experienced hardships because of his skin color. Nevertheless, he continued to have love and compassion toward everyone, even when those sentiments were not reciprocated. In one collection of sayings of the desert fathers, we have evidence of Moses' goodness despite negativity from others:

> Another day when a council was being held in Scetis, the Fathers treated Moses with contempt, in order to test him, saying, "Why does this black man come among us?" When Moses heard this, he kept silence. When the council was dismissed, they said to him, "Abba, did that not grieve you at all?" He said to them, "I am grieved, but I kept silence."[50]

Saint Moses the Black's life ended in 405 as the monastery was under attack by raiders. He encouraged the other monks to flee to safety, but Saint Moses remained along with a few other monks. All of these men met their martyrdom with him. Theirs was a life surrounded by honesty, love, mercy, prayer and compassion for all, even their persecutors.

SCRIPTURE

For surely I know the plans I have for you, says the LORD, plans for your welfare and not for harm, to give you a future with hope. Then when you call upon me and come and pray to me, I will hear you. When you search for me, you will find me; if you seek me with all your heart, I will let you find me, says the LORD, and I will restore your fortunes and gather you from all the nations and all the places where

I have driven you, says the LORD, and I will bring you back to the place from which I sent you into exile. (Jeremiah 29:11–14)

PRAYER

Dearest saint, you turned away from a life of villainy and murder to embrace the freedom and grace offered by the gospel. Your life mirrored the anger within all of us, but God's grace tempered you and allowed you to overcome the evils of your day. Thank you for making the seemingly impossible transition toward goodness a reality. Your example gives us hope, especially during the worst moments of our lives. Saint Moses the Black, be with us as we turn away from sin and live for the gospel. Amen.

REFLECTION

What measures can you use to expel the bad and adopt the good aspects of yourself? How do you know that God truly forgives the wrong you do? Must you do enough good to counteract the bad?

Saint of Chastity

Courage and commitment are the best words to describe the life of Blessed Anuarite. Her short life was marked with a struggle to maintain her virginity while living in a country torn by warfare and immorality. Because of her courage, Anuarite is remembered as a hero of the universal church.

Anuarite was born in what is now the Democratic Republic of the Congo to Christian parents who were very devoted to their children. Shortly after her baptism, she expressed a desire to become a Sister of the Holy Family. Her dream became a reality when she received her religious habit and the name Sister Marie Clementine Anuarite. Her only desire was to be a good sister, since this would certainly please God.

Anuarite was assigned to the classroom of her community's school. Although she was a firm and strict teacher, the girls loved her very much, often expressing unhappiness whenever Anuarite was absent due to poor health. Her love of the children in her care was evident. According to the book *Clementine Anuarite* by James Fanning, M.H.M., "Sometimes her superiors were a little worried when they saw her always in the company of the worst girls in the school but later she was able to show them that she was not trying to become like them but to win them back for Jesus."[51]

If the children loved Anuarite, her fellow sisters seemed to love her more. For them Anuarite was a priceless friend and true sister in Christ. Often she rushed to finish her chores so that she had time to assist another sister in

19

Blessed Marie Clementine Anuarite Nengapeta

=====

Virgin and Martyr

===

1941–1964

Feast Day
December 1

=

need. Even when novices had chores, Anuarite would assist them with the cooking, cleaning and other household duties. All of her actions earned Anuarite the love and respect of her sisters.

In 1964 the Congo experienced a period of civil war. During this time rebel soldiers took command and forced priests and religious from their homes. Anuarite's story becomes one of sadness and courageous resolve as the events that led to her violent death and the assault of the other religious sisters unfolded.

When the sisters were ordered to pack their things and leave the convent, they complied and were unaware of the true danger confronting them until the soldiers forced them onto a truck and began singing:

Oh the Little Wives of the Fathers
Where will they go tonight?
Oh! Oh! Oh! Each one of us will
have one for himself and amuse
himself this night![52]

These horrible words were an indication of the disrespect and imminent danger for the sisters. Certainly the nuns would need a miracle to survive their ordeal.

Unknown to Anuarite, the colonel in charge of the rebels had taken a liking to her. She was immediately ordered to the colonel who made repeated advances, but Anuarite insisted that he should stop, saying, "What you are asking is impossible. I cannot commit a sin. Kill me instead."[53] At that, the colonel snatched off her veil.

While the details of Anuarite's martyrdom are dramatic, they are real. Her final moments are recounted in her biography:

Sr. Anuarite and Sister Jean-Baptist Bokuma...were to get into the Volkswagen of Colonel Yuma Deo.... He forced the sisters into the back seat, but they went in one door and out the other. He tried several times but each time the sisters escaped. He started struggling with them and then started beating them with the butt of his gun.

Sr. Bokuma fell down with a broken arm. He set about Sr. Anuarite who tried to pull back "I don't want to commit this sin, if you want to, kill me. I forgive you because you don't know what you are doing." When the butt of the gun hit Anuarite's head, she said, "...this is just as I wanted it!"... His two henchmen took up positions over the body of Anuarite and started lunging into her chest with their big knives.... In all they must have stabbed her a dozen times and blood streamed out of the wounds. As she was still breathing, Olombe pulled out his revolver and aimed at her heart. One bullet went straight through her chest and killed her.[54]

The terror continued for another week until government forces caused the rebels to flee. The sisters searched until they found Anuarite's body and arranged for her burial.

Immediately word went out about this brave sister's sacrifice. Many were attracted to the faith because of her example of courage and chastity. In 1985 Pope John Paul II declared her blessed and asked all to support her cause for sainthood.

SCRIPTURE

So have no fear of them; for nothing is covered up that will not be uncovered, and nothing secret that will not become known. What I say to you in the dark, tell in the light; and what you hear whispered, proclaim from the housetops. Do not fear those who kill the body but cannot kill the soul; rather fear him who can destroy both soul and body in hell. Are not two sparrows sold for a penny? Yet not one of them will fall to the ground apart from your Father. And even the hairs of your head are all counted. So do not be afraid; you are of more value than many sparrows.

Everyone therefore who acknowledges me before others, I also will acknowledge before my Father in heaven; but whoever denies me before others, I also will deny before my Father in heaven. (Matthew 10:26–33)

PRAYER

Sister Anuarite, daughter of chastity, thank you for your model of virginity that is so dearly needed today. Your commitment can inspire us to remain pure for the Lord. Please watch over our young people, especially as they make decisions that affect their futures. Amen.

REFLECTION

All over the world, standards of chastity vary. What can you do in your community and by your example to present Christian standards of sexual purity to children as well as adults?

Saintly Children

The story of the precious lives of these young Ugandan martyrs is not well-known. These lay catechists were so young that we could correctly regard them as children, except for the fact that both children voluntarily walked into martyrdom. Both young men belonged to the Acholi tribe and were catechized by the Comboni Missionaries in 1915.

Daudi Okelo was born around 1902 to pagan parents in the village of Ogom-Payira. He received Christian instruction and baptism around age fourteen and immediately wanted to be a catechist. He could not wait to tell others about his new faith. In 1917 the local catechist died and Daudi petitioned the local priest, Father Cesare Gambaretto, for the position. This entailed going from village to village to instruct the people about the Catholic faith. Daudi was eager to get started, so Father Cesare assigned the young Jildo Irwa as his assistant.

Jildo Irwa was born around 1906 to pagan parents (his father would embrace the Catholic faith later) in the village of Bar-Kitoba. He was baptized by Father Cesare June 6, 1916, at about the age of ten. He and Daudi were confirmed on the same day, October 15, 1916.

Before the two young men set out for their first catechetical journey, Father Cesare spoke to them about their difficult assignment. Many of the villages were far apart, and there had been some local fighting and resentment about this new religion. But both young men could not be deterred from their mission. They set out in November or December of 1917.

20

Blesseds Daudi Okelo
and Jildo Irwa

=====

Catechists and Martyrs

===

d. 1918

=

In Paimol, the first village to where they journeyed, Daudi gathered the children for religious instruction and in a youthful manner, he and Jildo taught the children the prayers in the form of songs. Some of their songs were about the Blessed Virgin Mary, just so that the children could learn about her role as the mother of God. The two catechists went about their work with the serious dedication as any person committed to their mission. Each put their personalities into the work. According to the Vatican's biography, "Daudi of Payira is described as a young man of peaceful and shy character, diligent in his duties as a catechist and loved by all. He never got involved in tribal or political disputes...."[59] Father Cesare said, "Jildo was much younger than Daudi. Of lively and gentle nature...quite intelligent.... He was of great help to Daudi in gathering the children for the instruction with his gentle way and infantile insistence. He knew also how to entertain them with innocent village games and noisy and merry meetings."[60]

Both young men were martyred on the same day. They seemed to have had some warning because Daudi warned Jildo of possible danger. Jildo responded to this warning by saying, "Why should we be afraid? We have done nothing wrong to anyone; we are here only because Fr. Cesare sent us to teach the word of God. Do not fear!"[61]

Five people entered the boys' hut and told Daudi to stop his teaching. When he refused, they pierced him with their spears then threw his body onto a termite hill. The attackers then pierced Jildo with a spear, then another one hit him in the head with a knife. Daudi was sixteen and Jildo was twelve at the time of their martyrdom. They were so young, yet so devoted to a faith that was newly theirs. Pope John Paul II beatified these young people for their Christian witness and faithfulness to the gospel on October 20, 2002.

SCRIPTURE

People were bringing little children to him in order that he might touch them; and the disciples spoke sternly to them. But when Jesus saw this, he was indignant and said to them, "Let the little children come to me; do not stop them; for it is to such as these that the kingdom of God belongs. Truly I tell you, whoever does not receive the kingdom of God as a little child will never enter it." And he took them up in his arms, laid his hands on them, and blessed them. (Mark 10:13–16)

PRAYER

Blessed Daudi and Blessed Jildo, you were so young to embrace the faith so completely and devotedly. With sincere and innocent hearts, you accepted the roles of catechist and assistant catechist outside of your own village. In this light you agreed to venture to unknown people just to speak the Good News of the gospel. Without fear you happily instructed young people through song, prayers and repetition. Always peaceful, always young and diligent, always gentle and devoted, you two Ugandan wonders managed to widely witness the gospel to the people of your country with your eventual martyrdom. Pray for us that we may duplicate your sincerity and innocent devotion to the gospel. Amen.

REFLECTION

How can you, as an adult, recapture the youthful and innocent devotion to life and your faith? In what ways can you share this example with the young people entrusted to your care?

The Companion Saints

The passion of Perpetua and Felicitas in the year 203 was a remarkable expression of Christian sacrifice and courage and showed their willingness to model the essence of Jesus' command to "carry the cross and follow me" (Luke 14:27). Rarely has our church experienced a Christian bond as in the example of Felicitas and Perpetua of Carthage.

Saint Perpetua was a noblewoman of Carthage (in present-day Tunisia) and Felicitas was her slave. Both North African women were martyred in the arena for professing the Christian faith. We do not know a lot about Felicitas, only that she claimed to be a Christian while serving her mistress, Perpetua. We also know that she was expecting a baby at the time of her arrest but desperately desired martyrdom along with her companions. To this end, she successfully prayed to deliver her baby before the appointed arena date. Perpetua's diaries detail their imprisonment and give an up-close account of their path to martyrdom.

The diary portrays a commitment to the faith that causes others to admire the courage and friendship of these two women and their companions. At first they were under house arrest and could receive visitors. During one visit Perpetua's father attempted to persuade her away from the Christian faith. Perpetua recounts the conversation:

> While we were still under arrest (she said) my father out of love for me was trying to persuade me and shake my resolution.

21

Saints Perpetua
and Felicitas
=====
Noblewoman and Her Slave

===

d. 203
Feast Day
March 7

=

"Father," said I, "do you see this vase here, for example, or water-pot or whatever?"

"Yes, I do", said he.

And I told him: "Could it be called by any other name than what it is?"

And he said: "No."

"Well, so too I cannot be called anything other than what I am, a Christian."

At this my father was so angered by the word "Christian" that he moved towards me as though he would pluck my eyes out. But he left it at that and departed, vanquished along with his diabolical arguments.[55]

Perpetua's father was frantic about saving his well-bred daughter. It seems their family was influential and well-situated within Carthaginian society, as the family had slaves, land and position. His pleading with Perpetua failed to move his favorite child from her path to martyrdom.

Later they were moved to the arena prison at Carthage. Prison conditions were terrifying for the young women. Perpetua describes her terror and fear: "...I was terrified, as I had never before seen such a dark hole. What a difficult time it was! With the crowd the heat was stifling; then there was the extortion of the soldiers; and to crown all, I was tortured with worry for my baby there."[56]

Due to some supporters in the community, Perpetua and Felicitas were moved to a less crowded area of the prison where they were able to find slight comfort. Perpetua was also able to see her recently born baby, which brought comfort to both mother and child. These few pleasures made prison feel like a palace to Perpetua.

While in prison, Perpetua and Felicitas were baptized and managed to convert their guards to the faith. This level of commitment allowed these brave women an opportunity to prepare themselves for the arena and, ultimately, death, having to turn their backs on motherhood and their families. They wanted to devote all of their spiritual energy and prayers to their impending sacrifice. Neither woman nor any of their companions feared death; Perpetua's vision of heaven affirmed their resolve to die for the faith:

I saw a ladder of tremendous height made of bronze, reaching all the way to the heavens, but it was so narrow that only one person could climb up at a time. To the sides of the ladder were attached all sorts of iron weapons: there were swords, spears, hooks, daggers, and spikes; so that if anyone tried to climb up carelessly or without paying attention, he would be mangled and his flesh would adhere to the weapons.

At the foot of the ladder lay a dragon of enormous size, and it would attack those who tried to climb up and try to terrify them from doing so. And Saturus was the first to go up, he who was later to give himself up of his own accord. He had been the builder of our strength, although he was not present when we were arrested. And he arrived at the top of the staircase and he looked back and said to me: "Perpetua, I am waiting for you. But take care; do not let the dragon bite you."

...Then, using it as my first step, I trod on his head and went up.[57]

Perpetua had as many as four visions prior to her final torture in the arena. These proved to be a grace-filled gift that assured eternal glory to those steadfast in the faith.

Perpetua and Felicitas's passion in the arena was written down by eyewitnesses. This is one account of those final moments:

For the women the keepers had a savage cow ready, an unusual animal, chosen in mockery of their sex. They were stripped and wrapped in nets, and when they were thus brought out the people were shocked at the sight, the one a graceful girl, the other fresh from childbirth with milk dripping from her breasts. So they were brought back and clothed in loose gowns. First Perpetua was tossed. She sat up and drew her torn tunic about her, being more mindful of shame than of pain; and then she tidied her tumbled hair, for it was not seemly that a martyr should suffer with hair disheveled, lest she should appear to mourn in her glory. Then she got up and went to help [Felicitas], who had been knocked down.... Perpetua, "so lost...in the Spirit and ecstasy,"...asked when they were to be thrown to the cow. Only her bruises and torn dress persuaded her that it had already happened. Then she turned to her brother and another catechumen and said to them, "Stand fast in the faith and love one another. And do not let what we suffer be a stumbling-block to you."[58]

Perpetua and Felictas moved to the arena's center where the gladiators were waiting to kill them.

The unity and friendship that bonded Perpetua and Felicitas clearly witness the gospel qualities needed for us to take up our crosses and follow Jesus. Theirs was the martyrdom full of suffering, torture, separation and anxiety, but it was also a martyrdom filled with glory, promises, hope and salvation. It seems almost inappropriate to describe their passion from these two extremes, but this was the reality on their appointed day. Perpetua and Felicitas's final days on earth were marked with heroic suffering that became true glory in Christ.

SCRIPTURE
Now large crowds were traveling with him; and he turned and said to them, "Whoever comes to me and does not hate father and mother, wife and children, brothers and sisters, yes, and even life itself, cannot be my disciple. Whoever does not carry the cross and follow me cannot be my disciple." (Luke 14:25–27)

PRAYER
Perpetua and Felicitas, you spoke the courageous words of the gospel when others could not envision the Risen Lord. Throughout your ordeal, you remained women committed to salvation and eternal promises. Help us to remain faithful and courageous to the promises of Christ, just like you. In times of trouble, may we remember your examples of Christian virtue and trust in the Gospels. Amen.

REFLECTION
Can you identify ways to be a courageous Christian in today's world? What things hold you back from the love of God? What does the phrase "carry the cross and follow me" mean to you?

The Wise Saint

Good and wise Saint Poemen lived in the fifth century with his mother and brothers in Egypt. The brothers reportedly left home the same time as Poemen to enter a monastery, much to their mother's grief. Acknowledged as a "Desert Father," Poemen wrote the rules by which his community lived. His sayings reveal not only his wisdom, but also insight, experience, compassion and acceptance. Perhaps the best way to become acquainted with him is to experience some of these words of wisdom:

ON PROGRESS TO PERFECTION

Poemen said, "To be on guard, to meditate within, to judge with discernment; these are the three works of the soul."[62]

A brother asked him, "How ought we to live?" Poemen replied, "We have seen the example of Daniel. They accused him of nothing except that he served his God."[63]

Poemen said, "If a monk hates two things, he can be free of this world." A brother inquired, "What are they?" He said, "Bodily comfort and conceit."[64]

ON SELF-CONTROL

Poemen also said, "They smoke out bees in order to steal their honey. So idleness drives the fear of God from the soul, and steals its good works."[65]

ON NOTHING DONE FOR SHOW

Poemen also said, "Teach your heart to follow what your tongue is saying to others." He also said, "Men try to appear excellent

22

Saint Poemen
=====
Monk of Wisdom

===

Fifth Century
Feast Day
August 27

=

in preaching but they are less excellent in practising what they preach."[66]

ON NON-JUDGMENT

Joseph asked Poemen, "Tell me how to become a monk." He said, "If you want to find rest in this life and the next, say at every moment, 'Who am I?' and judge no one."[67]

A brother said to Poemen, "If I see my brother sin is it really right not to tell anyone about it?" He said, "When we cover our brother's sin, God covers our sin. When we tell people about our brother's guilt, God does the same with ours."[68]

ON HOSPITALITY

A brother came to Poemen in the second week of Lent and told him his thoughts, and found peace from his answer. Then he said, "I almost didn't come to see you today." Poemen asked him why. He said, "I was afraid that the door wouldn't be open as it is Lent." Poemen answered him, "It is not wooden doors we were taught to shut; the door we need to keep shut is the mouth."[69]

ON PATIENCE

Poemen said, "Whatever hardship comes upon you, it can be overcome by silence."[70]

As the authoritarian in the community, the other monks were obliged to bring their questions to Poemen, who answered with enough wisdom to lead the brothers to closer relationships with each other and with God.

SCRIPTURE

Listen, children, to a father's instruction,
    and be attentive, that you may gain insight;
For I give you good precepts:
    do not forsake my teaching.
When I was a son with my father,
    tender, and my mother's favorite,
he taught me, and said to me,
"Let your heart hold fast my words;
    keep my commandments, and live." (Proverbs 4:1–4)

PRAYER

Wise Saint Poemen, your life and sayings taught men to draw closer to God in the silence. Today you are still preaching your message of silence through your sayings. Help us, dear Saint Poemen, to realize that silence is still golden. Amen.

REFLECTION

From where do you draw adequate words to address the needs of your ever-changing community?

Persistent Lay Leader

23

Blessed Victoria Rasomanarivo

=====

Married Woman and Church Leader

===

1848–1894

Feast Day
August 21

=

The complete story of Blessed Victoria Rasomanarivo has yet to be told. All of the marvelously brave details of her life are not available. But what we do know must be told. It is important for the faith community to hear and say her name as we truly begin to understand her role in the Catholic church of Madagascar and how her actions ultimately impact the universal church as a whole.

This laywoman was born in 1848 to parents who worshiped according to their ancestral religion. At the age of fifteen Victoria was baptized a Christian much against her family's wishes. In fact, they threatened to turn their backs on her if she continued with the Christian faith. Despite their consistent threats, she embraced the faith even in light of her country's history of anti-Christian persecutions.

Although Christianity had been a part of Madagascar since the sixteenth century, it never replaced ancestral worship as the most practiced faith. In fact, in the year after Victoria's birth the persecution of Christians was ordered. Soldiers under Queen Ranavalona I captured over two thousand Christians, killing eighteen of them, burning four of them alive and throwing eighteen of them off a cliff two hundred feet to the ground. Ranavalona's son succeeded her and changed this persecution policy, favoring religious toleration, but his reign lasted only two years before he was assassinated. After his death the persecutions resumed.

Victoria's family continued to threaten her, but she remained unmovable in her Christian faith. According to Felicty O'Brien in *Saints in the Making*, they "found that she remained steadfast against all their threats and their pleas that she turn from Catholicism. The ultimate threat was that she would have to forfeit the right to be buried in the family tomb. This, in Malagasy society, was the worst form of rejection possible, the greatest punishment that could be given to anyone."[71]

When nothing could be done to stop Victoria from practicing Catholicism, the family arranged her marriage to the prime minister's son, thinking perhaps a husband could control this woman who refused to obey her family's wishes. Of course, this did not work. Victoria persisted in her routine of visiting the sick and poor, reciting the rosary and attending Mass.

She was a dutiful wife in all other respects, always honoring, respecting and serving her husband. This must have been hard for her as the husband chosen for Victoria was a drunken womanizer. He often brought other women home with him without considering Victoria's feelings or respecting her as his wife. Throughout the twenty-three years of their marriage, Victoria prayed for her husband. On his deathbed he was baptized. Perhaps his devoted wife's service to him and their community convinced him that a Christian countenance was the best way to meet death.

Victoria remained a pleasant, peaceful, happy and radiant person throughout her life. It seemed that nothing could deter her from the redeeming joy of being a Christian. This did not change in 1883 when the government threw Catholic priests out of Madagascar and locked the doors of all churches. The government's hope was that the church would dissolve without religious leadership. No one imagined that Victoria would stand up to the government and insist that the churches should remain open. Publicly she told officials, "You can put me to death, but you have no right to shut the church."[72] Because of her insistence, the churches eventually reopened. During the three years without priests, Victoria led the Catholic church in Madagascar. She made sure that religious instructions and Sunday prayers took place. Anyone accused being a Christian during the time of persecution had aid for their defense, and catechists received formal training to ensure that the church remained alive and vibrant. When the Jesuit priests returned, they were impressed with the organization, strength and spirit found in the local churches.

Blessed Victoria Rasomanarivo died in 1894 after a brief illness. Against her wishes she was buried in the family tomb. The family that had threatened with excluding her from this for so long now seemed eager to have her remains with them for eternity.

SCRIPTURE

Do not think that I have come to bring peace to the earth; I have not come to bring peace, but a sword.

For I have come to set a man against his father,
and a daughter against her mother,
and a daughter-in-law against her mother-in-law;
and one's foes will be members of one's own household.

Whoever loves father or mother more than me is not worthy of me; and whoever loves son or daughter more than me is not worthy of me; and whoever does not take up the cross and follow me is not worthy of me. Those who find their life will lose it, and those who lose their life for my sake will find it. (Matthew 10:34–39)

PRAYER

Blessed Victoria, you show us a life of total sacrifice for the gospel. In your life we see the loneliness and separation for all that would keep us from God's love. You risked it all: family, wealth, social position and even your own life. You decided to keep the church in Madagascar open regardless of the cost. Help us to realize the value of our own faith community so that we too can know God's goodness.

REFLECTION

If it seems your family is against you, how can you stand alone for what is right? How can you help keep the church alive when it seems so many are against it?

The Frugal Saint

Not much is known about Saint Serapion the Sedanite, but what we do know is amazing. Sources say he lived in Egypt as a slave. Saint Serapion was referred to as the Sedanite because of his one piece of clothing that he owned. During his lifetime Serapion sought to serve all in need.

The stories of his commitment to serve others are legendary. He continually sold his freedom in order to rescue others from a life of slavery. Once he did this for a twenty-cent debt. Another time he voluntarily became a slave to save a widow who owed a debt and was destitute.

In all of his positions as a slave, Saint Serapion remained prayerful and humbly devoted to his masters. His peaceful attitude and countenance affected his owners and resulted in their conversion to the faith. These conversions were especially notable when Saint Serapion was owned by a Manichean (one who advocated combining Gnosticism and Buddhism into a belief system where thought is reflected or found in cosmic reason). After serving him for ten years, the Manichean became a Catholic.

His commitment to the poor was exceptional from slavery to freedom to saint. He even sold the clothes his second master gave him in order to save another person.

Such was the amazing but true life of Saint Serapion the Sendanite, who presented to us a model for what it means to help the poor. His was the perfect picture of Jesus' command to love with your whole heart and being. After sixty years of service to others, Saint Serapion died in Egypt.

24

Saint Serapion the
Sendanite
=====
Egyptian Slave and Holy Man

===

dates unknown
Feast Day
August 26

=

SCRIPTURE

As he was setting out on a journey, a man ran up and knelt before him, and asked him, "Good Teacher, what must I do to inherit eternal life?" Jesus said to him, "Why do you call me good? No one is good but God alone. You know the commandments: "You shall not murder; You shall not commit adultery; You shall not steal; You shall not bear false witness; You shall not defraud; Honor your father and mother." He said to him, "Teacher, I have kept all these since my youth." Jesus, looking at him, loved him and said, "You lack one thing; go, sell what you own, and give the money to the poor, and you will have treasure in heaven; then come, follow me." When he heard this, he was shocked and went away grieving, for he had many possessions....

It is easier for a camel to go through the eye of a needle than for someone who is rich to enter the kingdom of God. (Mark 10:17–22, 25)

PRAYER

Dear Saint Serapion, we can only say, "Wow!" to the example of your life. Truly you desired a life devoted to others, a life of simple service to all. You lived Jesus' command to sell everything and follow him. Though you seemed poor by today's standards and those of your day, your actions to save others enriched all around you. Even your masters and companions were drawn to the gospel because of you and thereby gained eternal wealth. We thank you for such an example as you were truly a man for others. We pray for wisdom, trust and energy to do the same for family, friends and neighbors of our time. Amen.

REFLECTION

How far will you go to serve others? Where do you draw the line? When you read Jesus' command to follow him, what does this mean to you?

The First African Martyrs

On July 17 in the year 180 twelve Christians were arrested. Their names were Speratus, Nartzalus, Cittinus, Veturius, Felix, Aquilinus, Laetantius, Januaria, Generosa, Vestia, Donata and Secunda (who became known as the Scillitan Martyrs). It is important to note the martyrs' names specifically as too often names are lost. Also the fashion of saying, "and Companions" does not do justice to the martyrs who suffered for the faith. These twelve were the first recorded martyrs in Africa and their contribution to the universal church cannot be overlooked. From all accounts these events took place in Scillium, near Carthage (in present-day Tunisia).

Speratus, who spoke for the group, and his companions were brought before the Roman proconsul Publius Vigellius Saturninus. Of course, they were given the opportunity to renounce Christianity but refused. While being held captive, Speratus gave witness, "We have never committed any crime, we have injured no one; we have given thanks for the evil treatment we received, because we hold our own sovereign in honour."[73] His testimony caused the proconsul to question each of the Christians. This is a section of their additional testimonies:

> Speratus: "I do not recognize an empire of this world. Rather do I serve the God whom no man is able to see.... I recognize my master, the King of Kings and ruler of all peoples."

25

Saint Speratus and Companions
=====
First Christian Martyrs in Africa

===

Second Century
Feast Day
July 17

=

Saturninus, to the others: "Give up these beliefs."

Speratus: "That we should do murder or bear false witness, that is the evil belief."

Saturninus: "Do not share in this lunacy."

...

Vestia: "I am a Christian."

Secunda: "So am I, and I want to be nothing else."

...

"Will you take time to think about it?" asked the proconsul.

Speratus: "There is nothing to think about when what is right is so clear."

Saturninus: "What have you got in your case?"

Speratus: "The Books, and the letters of a righteous man called Paul."[74]

All of them insisted that they were Christians and nothing else. The proconsul then sentenced each to death. They all reportedly responded, "Thanks be to God."

In the second century it must have been somewhat of a surprise to be arrested for being a Christian. Speratus and his companions were not criminals; they had done nothing to break any civil or moral laws. As the first martyrs in Africa they might not have known that their arrest would lead to death. Being the first to experience this harsh anti-Christian treatment, how did they really feel? What were their first thoughts? We do not know, but thanks be to God for their sacrifice and testimony.

Perhaps the words of Speratus can speak to us in our twenty-first–century world: "...what is right is so clear."

SCRIPTURE

But by the grace of God I am what I am, and his grace toward me has not been in vain. On the contrary, I worked harder than any of them—though it was not I, but the grace of God that is with me. (1 Corinthians 15:10)

PRAYER

You were all martyrs, the first African martyrs! Saying that you were Christians and carrying Paul's books around with you were pious actions. But being a martyr so early in the church constitutes bravery and true faithfulness. In the second century the church was still early in its development, yet you thanked God for your martyrdom. Saints Speratus, Nartzalus, Cittinus, Veturius, Felix, Aquilinus, Laetantius, Januaria, Generosa, Vestia, Donata and Secunda, you simply said that you were Christians. No one else in Africa had proclaimed this so clearly as you. Please pray for us, that each of us can simply say, I am a Christian too. Amen.

REFLECTION

Are you ever hesitant or neglectful about professing your faith? When has this happened to you? When you are around others from another faith and they speak about their church activities and events, do you chime in with your activities? Do you make your faith known to others?

26

Blessed Cyprian Michael Iwene Tansi

=====

Priest and Monk

===

1903–1964

Feast Day
January 20

=

The Reconciliation Saint

From all accounts Father Cyprian Michael Iwene Tansi led a very holy and peaceful life. He was born of Igbo parents who worshiped the local Nigerian gods. But they sent Cyprian to the mission schools, which taught him the Catholic faith. When he was baptized into the Catholic church at age nine, he stopped practicing his former faith and destroyed an idol given to him at birth. This was a clear sign to his parents and family members that he had become a Catholic forever. Cyprian must have been a very advanced student because he began teaching at age sixteen and entered the seminary six years later. During his years of ordained life, Father Tansi consistently worked to bring all men and women closer to God, especially through the sacraments.

He was ever obedient, even when asked to leave his homeland to study Trappist spirituality in the hopes of bringing this way of life back to Nigeria. Father Tansi accepted this task and journeyed to England where he spent fourteen years preparing to bring the contemplative life back to Africa. Father Tansi never lost his faith in God nor his prayerful countenance, especially after the Trappists changed the site of their proposed monastery from Nigeria to Cameroon. Nevertheless, he continued to prepare himself for his new mission as a Trappist monk.

In 1963 Father Tansi left England for Cameroon to begin his duties as a novice master. A year later he was forced to return to England for medical treatment due to an aortic aneurysm. He died a few weeks later. Though small, seemingly frail and blind in one eye,

Father Tansi had shepherded his people directly to the source of all peace, the Lord. In a 1959 letter to his houseboy he wrote:

> Yourself and your wife should always keep before your eyes that fact that you are creatures, God's own creation. As a man's handiwork belongs to him, so do we all belong to God, and should accordingly have no other will but his.... Leave yourself in His hands, not for a year, not for two years, but as long as you live on earth. If you confide in Him fully and sincerely He will take special care of you.[75]

That same year he wrote to Augustine Chendo, one of his parishioners, and shared: "Prayer is the best weapon for obtaining favors from God. Pray, pray often, pray with all your heart, pray to God, pray to our Blessed Mother. Mass is the most powerful of all prayers."[76]

Too many people outside of Nigeria are unfamiliar with this truly gifted priest. Pope John Paul II spoke eloquently about this holy man at the Mass of his beatification. From the following text, we learn about Father Tansi's devotion to all of God's people:

> The life and witness of Father Tansi is an inspiration to everyone in the Nigeria that he loved so much. He was first of all a man of God: his long hours before the Blessed Sacrament filled his heart with generous and courageous love. Those who knew him testify to his great love of God. Everyone who met him was touched by his personal goodness. He was then a man of the people: he always put others before himself, and was especially attentive to the pastoral needs of families. He took great care to prepare couples well for Holy Matrimony and preached the importance of chastity. He tried in every way to promote the dignity of women. In a special way, the education of young people was precious to him....
>
> He encouraged people to confess their sins and receive God's forgiveness in the Sacrament of Reconciliation.... He spread the joy of restored communion with God.[77]

This humble saintly spirit was beatified so that all the world could know about his wonderful impact on the universal church.

SCRIPTURE

And the Lord's servant must not be quarrelsome but kindly to everyone, an apt teacher, patient, correcting opponents with gentleness. (2 Timothy 2:24–25a)

PRAYER

Dear Father Tansi, peacemaker to all, the world celebrated with the Nigerian community as your cause for sainthood was presented. Your quiet strength has affected those who participate in evangelization programs like RCIA and pre-Cana. We know and appreciate that you valued sacramental preparation, in particularly the preparation for the sacrament of matrimony. We pray that others will be encouraged too so that our church may build a powerful spirit in the name of the Lord. Thank you for your example of patient endurance for the people of God. Amen.

REFLECTION

What role can you play in parish evangelization programs? If you take a moment to evaluate parish needs and your own abilities, how can you facilitate or develop new parish programs?

The Repentant Saint

Thais, a prostitute from Alexandria, became very wealthy because of her trade. It seems that she was quite famous throughout the Alexandrian community. Although many historians question the truth of her story, many people accept the story as fact centuries after her death. The details are a bit sketchy and there are no written texts to corroborate the events around her life, but hagiographers explain her life as one completely turned around by the Gospels. It seems that Saint Paphnitius, a disciple of Saint Antony, eventually convinced Thais that she must return to her Christian upbringing and repent. When Paphnitius asked to privately speak with Thais, she remarked, "What do you fear?... If you fear men, we are private here. If you fear God there is no place to hide from Him."[78] This was evidence that she was aware of God's commandments and the Risen Lord.

There are conflicting accounts as to what happened after her conversion. Some accounts say that she burned all of her jewels and elements of wealth and that Paphnitius walled her up in a monastery, only releasing her on Saint Antony's advice. Another account reports that she gave all of her wealth to the poor and stayed in a solitary cell in a monastery because she did not deem herself worthy of contact with other nuns. Whatever really happened, we know that Saint Thais had the opportunity to repent for her sins. After being holed up for three years, eating only bread and drinking water, she ended her solitude and merged her life with the

27

Saint Thais
=====
Prostitute and Religious

===

Fourth Century
Feast Day
October 8

=

other religious sisters in the monastery. Unfortunately, she died fifteen days later.

How sad that we do not have any writings from this great woman of faith. She must have had some words of wisdom to impart to us after living such a notorious lifestyle, then being confined for so long. Her story definitely merits more discussion and research by hagiographers everywhere.

SCRIPTURE

The scribes and the Pharisees brought a woman who had been caught in adultery; and making her stand before all of them, they said to him, "Teacher, this woman was caught in the very act of committing adultery. Now in the law Moses commanded us to stone such women. Now what do you say?" They said this to test him, so that they might have some charge to bring against him. Jesus bent down and wrote with his finger on the ground. When they kept on questioning him, he straightened up and said to them, "Let anyone among you who is without sin be the first to throw a stone at her." And once again he bent down and wrote on the ground. (John 8:3–8)

PRAYER

Good and worthy Saint Thais, no one can deny you the love of our precious Lord! Though you led a sinful beginning, you turned your life around by embracing the faith. Honestly, who among us is without sin? When you embraced the gospel, you did as Jesus instructed the rich, to give to the poor and follow him. Saint Thais, pray for us that we may be found worthy of Christ's many promises. Amen.

REFLECTION

Do you feel a certain way toward those with lifestyles different than your own (prostitutes, criminals, even the poor)? Is your attitude one of hatred, compassion, superiority or something else? How can you model your own sinful life after Saint Thais by changing direction and repenting?

The Newlywed Saints

Timothy and Maura's story of a gruesome martyrdom is brief but so loving and full of commitment that it must be included in this book. The virtues of love and commitment permeate these events but seem lost on our world today. We need their example and more like it to restore relationships between husbands and wives, parents and children, friends and our entire society.

Timothy and Maura were newlyweds (married for about twenty days) when Timothy, a lector at the church at Penapolis, near the ancient city of Antinoe, Egypt, was ordered to turn over the sacred texts of the church to Roman authorities during Emperor Diocletian's persecutions of Christians. Timothy refused to comply and was arrested and tortured by soldiers who poked a red-hot iron rod into his ears and cut off his eyelids. Timothy persisted in his refusal to turn over the sacred texts. The officials then sent for his wife, Maura, attempting to convince Timothy to turn over the books. When Maura arrived she urged her husband to remain firm, and she also was arrested. The soldiers ripped out the hair from Maura's head, and then both Timothy and Maura were nailed to a wall where they remained suffering for nine days, during which they gave each other encouragement, before dying.

Their story shows us how dedicated both martyrs were to each other as well as the faith. Nothing would deter them from protecting the church and the faithful.

28

Saints Timothy
and Maura
=====
Married Martyrs

===

d. ca. 298
Feast Day
May 3

=

SCRIPTURE

Only, live your life in a manner worthy of the gospel of Christ, so that, whether I come and see you or am absent and hear about you, I will know that you are standing firm in one spirit, striving side by side with one mind for the faith of the gospel.... (Philippians 1:27)

PRAYER

Saints Timothy and Maura, though married for only a short time, your devotion to each other as well as the gospel was remarkable. Turning over the sacred texts seemed an easy option to protect your lives, but you refused to give these precious documents to authorities. By this refusal, your lives were cruelly ended. Your martyrdom afforded you both an opportunity to stand up for what is right. Through your witness, help us to stand for what is right as well. Amen.

REFLECTION

Have you ever said or done something wrong just to make a situation less frightening or upsetting? Once the tension ended, how did you feel?

Man of Charity

Pierre Toussaint's life really is a remarkable one that leaves you saying, "That's incredible." It is hard to believe that a man would remain enslaved just because his widowed owner needed him. It is also a stretch to understand how one man could endure racial indignities, even in his church, yet continue to nurture his Catholic spirit of philanthropy and good will. How does such a person manage to remain positive amid every obstacle and emerge as a pillar of courage and strength both for his oppressors and supporters? These were the remarkable aspects of Pierre Toussaint's life.

Toussaint was born into slavery in Haiti around 1766. He was reared by his mother and grandmother, both Catholic women who passed the faith on to Pierre and his sister, Rosalie. In addition to religious matters, Pierre also knew how to read, write and play the violin. His master insisted that Pierre receive a good education, as he planned that Pierre would be a tutor for his own children.

When a revolution broke out in Haiti, Pierre's owner, Jean Berard, moved his family and slaves to New York City. While in New York Pierre learned the hairdressing trade and mastered every technique, which ultimately placed him in high demand by the most wealthy and influential women. Later these clients would join Pierre in his charity efforts.

Jean Berard eventually traveled to Haiti to check on his assets there, only to die shortly after returning to New York.

As a hairdresser to the wealthy, Pierre, though still a slave, was able to support his mistress and begin his philanthropic work. For forty

29

Venerable Pierre
Toussaint
=====
Slave, Hairdresser and
Universal Philanthropist

===

1766–1853
Feast Day
June 30

=

years he supported Saint Elizabeth Ann Seton with her orphanage. He sent aid to the Oblate Sisters of Providence to maintain their work among the black community in Baltimore. He opened a school in New York City to educate black children, the first in the city. He assisted other Haitian refugees, helping to provide them with food, clothing and shelter. He tended the victims of a yellow fever epidemic.

In addition to his wealthy clients, Pierre Toussaint had support from his wife, Juliette Noel, whom he married after becoming emancipated (Mrs. Berard freed Pierre on her deathbed), and his daughter, Euphemia (Rosalie's child), whom he adopted after her mother's death. They became his joy during the harsh times of racial hatred. Even though Pierre assisted every segment of society regardless of race, he still faced discrimination because of his skin color. He was proud of being black and of being Catholic and was known for "a quiet wit and gaiety" and an ability to be discreet.[79]

In 1853 this servant of God died and was buried next to Juliette and Euphemia in Old St. Patrick's Cemetery in New York City. In 1968 his process for canonization was begun by Cardinal John O'Connor, archbishop of New York. As his cause was under way, Pierre Toussaint's remains were moved in 1990 to a crypt under the main altar at St. Patrick's Cathedral. He is the only layperson buried at the prestigious cathedral. In 1996 Pope John Paul II declared him venerable. A miracle is still needed for his beatification and another for his canonization.[80]

SCRIPTURE

When reviled, we bless; when persecuted, we endure; when slandered, we speak kindly. (1 Corinthians 4:12b–13a)

PRAYER

Pierre Toussaint, how did you have the compassion, strength and patience to survive slavery and the evil of your day? You were willing to serve others, even when others hated and despised you. You loved those close to you, but how did you love your enemies too? Please teach us your ways of responsibility, generosity and kindness toward all men and women. Amen.

REFLECTION

How can you open your heart enough to love your enemies? What is the message of service throughout the lives of the saints saying to your community?

Warrior for the Faith

Pope Saint Victor I led the church at a time of great heresies and debates. He was pope while the debate about when Catholics should celebrate Easter was under way. It seemed that the church in the East celebrated Easter on the fourteenth day of the Jewish month of Nisan or on the Feast of Passover. The advocates of this date were known as Quartodecimans, from the Latin for "fourteenth day." When Victor I proposed Sunday as the acceptable time for Easter celebration, the churches in Asia Minor objected.

Victor's papacy was plagued with fights—fights he picked as he refused to let any teaching he believed was a heresy to go unchallenged. Some of these heresies included:

Adoptionists: Believed that Jesus was purely human, not divine. They professed that Jesus was adopted by God.

Gnostics: Believed salvation was obtained through the accumulation of knowledge, not by the will of God.

Monarchianists: Denied the distinct divine personhood of Jesus and the Holy Spirit.

We should still view Victor's leadership as a positive papacy despite these constant squabbles with heretics. He is credited with being the first pope to communicate with the Roman Empire. This is significant as Victor I influenced the release of many condemned Christians. He is also noted as a martyr, though no evidence exists to support this papal martyrdom.

30

Pope Saint Victor I

=====

The Fifteenth Pope

===

r. 189–ca. 198

Feast Day
July 28

=

SCRIPTURE

Whoever welcomes you welcomes me, and whoever welcomes me welcomes the one who sent me. Whoever welcomes a prophet in the name of a prophet will receive a prophet's reward; and whoever welcomes a righteous person in the name of a righteous person will receive the reward of the righteous.... (Matthew 10:40–41)

PRAYER

Dear Pope Victor, you were quite faithful to take on these great battles. The safety of the church was at stake and you championed its cause with a positive spirit. Settling the Easter debate was a major hurdle, after all, who could imagine Easter on any other day but Sunday, the Lord's Day? Dear Saint Victor, help us to be more faithful, especially in times of turmoil. Amen.

REFLECTION

In what ways do you evaluate and accept changes within the church? How do you process the change? How can you become the peacemaker during change?

Part Two
Saints in Waiting

Orphans' Advocate

31

Mother Mathilda Beasley

=====

Religious

===

1832–1903

=

This generous woman was born Mathilde Taylor on November 14, 1832. Her mother, Caroline, was a slave, and her father is thought to have been a Native American named James Taylor. The facts are sketchy about Mathilde's (later she began spelling this as Mathilda) young years in New Orleans and how she received her freedom from James Taylor, who owned both her and her mother. It is clear, however, that Mathilda was in Savannah, Georgia, by 1859 teaching African American children, which she had to keep secret because at the time "punishment for teaching slaves or free person of color to read" was a "fine and whipping."[81] Since there are no records of her school, she must have been successful at keeping the school and her mission there a secret.

In 1869 Mathilda married Abraham Beasley, a freed black who seemed to be a well-to-do businessman in Savannah. Abraham owned a restaurant, market, saloon and boardinghouse. He also owned additional land throughout Savannah. Their marriage was short-lived as Abraham died in 1877, leaving his estate to Mathilda. She should have been financially secure with this estate and no children to care for, but Mathilda saw a need within her community and decided to donate her wealth to establish the St. Francis Home for Colored Orphans in Savannah. She then traveled to England to become a Catholic religious.

On her return to Savannah, Mathilda Beasley founded the Third Order of St. Francis, Georgia's first religious order of black sisters. Her community's mission was to educate and nurture the orphans of Georgia. This was no easy mission as the sisters were faced with hatred still present from slavery and the ill effects of the Civil War. They were still working to overcome this twenty-six years after the Emancipation Proclamation and twenty-four years after the Civil War. Despite the legal emancipation, black and white relations were still poor, and the orphanage was subjected to arson and eventually financial ruin.

She did receive financial support from Cardinal James Gibbons of Baltimore and Katharine Drexel of Philadelphia (now Saint Katharine Drexel). In fact, when Mother Beasley wrote to Cardinal Gibbons requesting assistance, she said, "for my community is so very small. If your Eminence can send me a few subjects, it will be one of the greatest helps for this Mission. Then we could work to help ourselves."[82] Directly after this communication, Mother Mathilda approached the Sisters of the Blessed Sacrament outside of Philadelphia for additional spiritual aid for her community. Mother Mathilda and her sisters considered going to Pennsylvania to receive formation training, but eventually decided against it.

Mother Mathilda continued to struggle to obtain more sisters to staff the orphanage and support her small community. She continued to write to Mother Katharine as well as Father John Slattery of the Josephites in Baltimore. Her main concern was for more vocations and this was her plea in every letter. Finally, in May of 1897 the community was suppressed due to the lack of vocations. The sisters as well as Mother Beasley returned to a life among the laity. Mother Beasley continued to support the orphans through fund-raising and sewing. Upon her death in 1903, she was found in a posture of prayer before a statue of the Blessed Virgin.

On the surface it would seem that Mathilda Beasley's mission was a complete failure. Yes, her congregation was suppressed and she died alone after years of frustrating work within the church, but her message of love, care and undying faith in our cause as Catholics continues to live on. Her life gave witness to the merits of educating African American children and the value of an African American presence in the Catholic church. Mother Mathilda's obituary read, "Protestants speak in the highest terms of her life and character, and among the negroes the feeling prevails that they have lost the best and truest friends and benefactors"[83] She has been honored with a park near her home as well as a historical marker to commemorate her sacrifice for the people of Savannah.

SCRIPTURE

The steadfast love of the LORD never ceases,
    his mercies never come to an end;
they are new every morning;
    great is your faithfulness.
"The LORD is my portion," says my soul,
    "therefore I will hope in him." (Lamentations 3:22–24)

PRAYER

Mother Beasley, you gave everything to nurture and educate the orphans of Savannah. This sacrifice was great and worthy to be remembered as an effort of self-sacrifice. Although some view your work as a failure, God and many others know the true valiant success within you. Our church and world needs more believers such as you. Amen.

REFLECTION

What are you doing for the children around you? If you are not working directly with children, how can your attitudes and actions be a model of faith for young observers?

Smiling and Celebrating Sister

Well, that's really it! If you add a little movement and attitude and spirit and wonderfulness
and humor and smiling and God's radiance,
that would be close to yelling: Thank the good
Lord for sending Sister Thea our way! Her story
has already been told well in other documen-
taries and books, but this great saint must be
included in this book.

Bertha Bowman was born in Yazoo City,
Mississippi, in 1937. None of her family members were Catholic, but she was attracted to the
faith in the 1940s when Catholic missionaries
came to Yazoo City. She heard the singing and
wanted to know "what was going on and had
heard that the Catholics worship statues."[84]
When Thea was twelve her parents enrolled her
in Holy Child Jesus Catholic School after they
discovered that she had not learned how to read
at the public school. Four years later Bertha
Bowman entered the Franciscan Sisters of
Perpetual Adoration (FSPA) in LaCrosse,
Wisconsin, taking the name Thea, meaning "of
God," in honor of her father, Theon.

She was the only African American sister in
the community, but she didn't let that stop her.
Thea knew she had to change her eating habits
and overall lifestyle, but she didn't mind as long
as she could be the best sister possible.
Whatever it took to be the best, she would do it
happily.

As an FSPA, one of Sister Thea's challenges
was to promote awareness among black Catholics
of their role in the church. Her message tells us
that black Catholics bring a rich heritage to the
universal church that should be recognized:

32

Sister Thea Bowman
=====
Religious

===

1937–1990

=

What does it mean to be a black and Catholic? It means that I come to my church fully functioning. That doesn't frighten you, does it? I come to my church fully functioning. I bring myself, my black self, all that I am, all that I have, all that I hope to become, I bring my whole history, my traditions, my experience, my culture, my African-American song and dance and gesture and movement and teaching and preaching and healing and responsibility as gift to the church.[85]

Certainly she gives us plenty to talk about and sing about and shout about. Many people asked, "Why is Sister Thea so happy?" "What's she singing about now?" To understand Thea, first just look at her. With those sparkling eyes and warm smile, she must have been up to something good. People always wanted to be around Thea, to listen to her message and to share in the joy. We hear this joy in her songs and observe it in her dance. We emerge from our time with Sister Thea covered with hope, hope that the Lord will take care of whatever we need. We walk away hopeful, filled with her shared joy because we are reminded that Jesus is indeed with us.

Even though diagnosed with breast cancer in 1987, Sister Thea continued to sing and inspire us. She makes us want to sing, too. She makes us want to shout just like her, "I'm a child of God!" Sister Thea was actually a ball of energetic smiling light, urging us to celebrate because we were children of God. Until the end of her days, Sister Thea joyfully encouraged African-Americans to celebrate their possibilities.

SCRIPTURE

Make a joyful noise to the Lord, all the earth.
> Worship the Lord with gladness;
> come into his presence with singing.

Know that the Lord is God.
> It is he that made us, and we are his;
> we are his people, and the sheep of his pasture.

Enter his gates with thanksgiving,
> and his courts with praise.
> Give thanks to him, bless his name.

For the Lord is good;
> his steadfast love endures for ever,
> and his faithfulness to all generations. (Psalm 100)

PRAYER

Sister Thea, you taught us to celebrate our possibilities. When things looked bleak, you showed us how to sing a song of joy or to think about God's goodness. It was you, the one with the smiling presence, who urged us to pull together, to hold onto God's promises, to have hope and to truly live until we die. Always your energy enticed us to be children of God and unified through the gospel. Dear Sister Thea, please pray for us so that we can know your song of strength and joy! Amen.

REFLECTION

What are you singing about these days? When you think about your possibilities, what are you celebrating?

Seruant of Seruants

We thank God that Henriette Delille refused to accept the requirements of her day! We thank God that she was a woman willing to seek out only what God called her to do.

Henriette Delille was born in New Orleans in 1812 to a free black woman, Marie Joseph Diaz (called Pouponne) and a wealthy white French, businessman, Jean Baptiste Delille-Sarpy. Her parents were never married, as it was illegal for interracial marriages to exist in the United States.

Jean Baptiste provided for his children as they were educated, dressed well and supported with his financial resources. Pouponne Diaz was independent to a degree as she provided natural medicines and assistance to those in need. Often Henriette was expected to help her mother with the special herbs and bandages. In this role Henriette saw many slaves who had been beaten by their masters and other whites. She couldn't believe that one person should have such power over another, but she was happy to offer whatever care possible. Henriette did not know it, but her medical skills would come in handy as she altered the plans already in motion for her future.

As a free woman of color, Henriette was expected to attend the Quadroon Ball like all of the women in her family before her. This was a special event in which free women of color had a chance to meet the young, influential white gentlemen of New Orleans. Such men financed the balls themselves, charging ticket prices high enough to keep out less desirables. Henriette's mother had attended a Quadroon Ball, as did

33

Henriette Delille

=====

Religious

===

1812–1862

=

her sister, Cecile, and soon it would be Henriette's turn to look for love and security at the Quadroon. Unknown to Henriette's family, she had other thoughts about her future.

When Pouponne was called to attend to a young girl, Henriette accompanied her and met a French religious named Sister Saint Marthe Fortiere. Sister Saint Marthe opened a school for free people of color, so she taught free children by day and slave children by night. This arrangement fascinated Henriette. She soon began to teach the children about God. In providing religious instruction, Henriette also taught the slaves how to read. This was illegal, but she continued.

Henriette met Juliettte Gaudin and the two nursed the slaves, fed the poor and continued to teach people of color. They both recognized their desire for a prayerful life in service to those in need. In 1836 these women joined Marie-Jeanne Aliquot, a wealthy Frenchwoman, and Josephine Charles, a free woman of color, to form the Sisters of the Presentation of the Blessed Virgin Mary, but this small group of laywomen soon disbanded.

Henriette's vision would soon be realized when Father Etienne Rousselon came to New Orleans in 1837. The French priest admired the work of Henriette, Josephine, Marie-Jeanne and Juliette among the slaves and colored population of New Orleans. He agreed to assist them in establishing a religious order to serve the slaves and free people of color. By 1842 this promise of assistance became a reality as the Sisters of the Holy Family were founded.

Henriette and her sisters continued to perform works of charity for the people of New Orleans, even amid the harsh insults that they endured because of their work and their color. These indignities continued until 1853 when the yellow fever epidemic swarmed through New Orleans. The sisters nursed all victims (white and black, slave and free) without regard for their own safety. Their efforts gained approval from New Orleans citizens and alleviated some of the social stigma of belonging to the religious community of black women.

Henriette Delille lived in ill health for another nine years and died of pleurisy at the age of fifty. Her obituary read, "she had, for the love of Jesus Christ, become the humble and devoted servant of the slaves."[86] In 1989 Archbishop Francis B. Schulte of New Orleans suggested that it was time to pursue her cause for canonization.

In the history of the Catholic church, Henriette Delille remains an example of one who provided true love and service to the people of God. If ever anyone lived the gospel, she certainly did.

PRAYER FOR THE BEATIFICATION OF HENRIETTE DELILLE
O good and gracious God, you called Henriette Delille to give herself in service and in love to the slaves and the sick, to the orphan and the aged, to the forgotten and the despised. Grant that inspired by her life we might be renewed in heart and mind. If it be your will, may she one day be raised to the honor of sainthood. By her prayers may we live in harmony and peace. Through Jesus Christ our Lord, Amen.[87]

SCRIPTURE
Your kingdom is an everlasting kingdom,
    and your dominion endures throughout all generations.

The LORD is faithful in all his words,
    and gracious in all his deeds.
The LORD upholds all who are falling,
    and raises up all who are bowed down.
The eyes of all look to you,
    and you give them their food in due season.
You open your hand,
    satisfying the desire of every living thing. (Psalm 145:13–16)

PRAYER
How did you turn against the expectation of your time? What courage emanated from you to reproach slave owners and the systems of oppression that they endorsed. You and your friends were so few, yet you insisted on teaching all people, both slave and free. It seems that you did so much as you established the Sisters of the Holy Family. Please, Mother Henriette, help us to be courageous like you. Amen.

REFLECTION
What would motivate someone in your community to give everything away and help the poor?

An Eager Servant

Augustine Derricks fostered an extreme antagonism toward the Catholic church as a young Protestant boy in San Domingo in the West Indies. He came to the United States in 1904 to study for the Protestant ministry and to fight the Catholic church. He studied at Howard University in Washington, D.C., where he had the occasion to continue his hatred of the Catholic church. One day he visited a Catholic family in Washington and had the experience of learning some elements of the Catholic faith from the child who lived in the house. Augustine was so moved with her honesty that he began an investigation into the faith. He began instructions within a year and was soon baptized.

Such was Augustine's eagerness to embrace the Catholic faith that he soon knew that God was calling him to the priestly life. The only problem would be to find a seminary willing to accept colored candidates for ordination. His quest was a failure within the United States but the Trinitarians welcomed Augustine to their novitiate at Livorno in Tuscany, Italy. In 1921 he received the habit and one year later professed vows and moved to Rome to study theology and philosophy. Father Augustine of the Ascension, as Augustine was now known, must have been a fast learner because not only did he master philosophy and theology, but he became fluent in five languages as well. Eventually the Trinitarians sent Father Augustine to St. Ann's Parish in Bristol, Pennsylvania. This was an Italian parish where Father Augustine fit right in as he was fluent in Italian. The pastor of St.

34

Father Augustine
Derricks
=====
Priest

===

1887–1929

=

109

Ann's encouraged his new assistant to accept speaking engagements across the country to promote vocations. It was clear that vocations to the priesthood and religious life were a primary concern for Father Augustine as well as the Trinitarians. His role as assistant pastor allowed time for these speaking and collaboration events with Fathers Augustus Tolton, John Dorsey, Charles Uncles and Joseph John, the four other African American priests in the United States.

Father Augustine was well-known to the Sisters of the Blessed Sacrament in Pennsylvania as well as to anyone concerned about black vocations and evangelization efforts. Black Catholics in Pennsylvania as well as around the country flocked to any place where Father Augustine preached or was present. They were eager to see the man of color who desperately wanted to be a priest for God and an example to his people. He exuded a sense of piety and possessed a straightforward attitude about the faith and the church.

The excitement of experiencing this wonderful servant of God was short-lived as Father Augustine died in 1929, only two years after ordination, from complications related to appendicitis and surgery. Father Augustine of the Ascension was buried in St. Mark's Cemetery in Bristol after the funeral liturgy at St. Ann's Church in Bristol, Pennsylvania. It is interesting to note that none of the other African American priests were in attendance but the church was, in fact, crowded with people of color.

The headline in the *Catholic Standard and Times* read "Colored Priest, Rev. A. Derricks, Trinitarian, Dies. Was One of Four in United States—Became Convert to Church and Was Ordained in Rome in 1927."[88] Father Vincent Dever said the funeral Mass, which highlighted the need for vocations among the people of color in the United States. He spent time preaching about the need for vocations because Father Augustine emphasized this at every occasion. Father Dever remarked:

> There is absolutely no room for doubt of the need of Colored priests. We know this from the nature of the case. They will have better understanding of the needs, the difficulties and the temperament of their own people, and their mode of thought will be the same. This will clearly give them a great advantage in getting a hearing from them and in winning them the true faith. We

know it from history. Every people has had its own priests, and it has been its own priests that have done the greatest part in making and keeping any people constant in the faith.[89]

Let us remember Father Augustine Derricks and his requests for vocations among the African American Catholic community.

SCRIPTURE

Then I heard the voice of the Lord saying, "Whom shall I send, and who will go for us?" And I said, "Here am I; send me!" (Isaiah 6:8)

PRAYER

Dear Father Derricks, you wanted to be a priest so badly. The warm and confident smile of yours let others know that you were happy with the priesthood because of the peace and joy seeping into your life. Please help our young people know the excitement of wanting something so desperately for God. Amen.

REFLECTION

How are you promoting vocations to the priesthood and religious life? Are you asking or inspiring your own children to consider serving God in this way?

Catholic Explorer

John-Baptiste Pointe du Sable's gifts to the black Catholic community are significant as are his sacrifices for the history of the United States of America. This trapper and settler's background before entering the Mississippi River Valley is uncertain. Until the end of the eighteenth century, we can only guess about his beginnings. One historian suggests that this saint-in-waiting probably arrived in the Illinois area from Canada or from southern Louisiana, probably after leaving Haiti.

We do, however, know that du Sable was the first to settle the region now known as Chicago. He was a free man who owned land in Illinois and had a spacious residence in the area. This was one of his significant contributions because the eighteenth century offered few opportunities for blacks to own land in America. He must have possessed more than adequate financial resources to accomplish the task of purchasing and maintaining land.

As a Catholic pioneer, du Sable overcame the prejudice of his day that prohibited blacks from having marriages blessed by the church. In 1788 he married a Potowatomi woman named Catherine. They were married by a Catholic priest and proceeded to raise a family within the Catholic church.

Though wonderful events seemed to follow Jean-Baptiste Pointe du Sable, this was not the case. We must remember that he was a pioneer, a pacesetter, a first in many regards. His life couldn't have been easy as he paved the way against prejudice (against both blacks and Native Americans) and hatred. Even as he faced

---

35

Jean-Baptiste Pointe du Sable

=====

Trapper, Settler, Friend to the Native Americans

===

1745–1818

=

the American people with their ideas of a black man's limitations, the British troops captured du Sable and threw him into prison because of his friendship with the Native American populations.

Du Sable's life ended on a less-than-glorious note as he was forced into poverty at the end of his life. In 1800 he sold everything to his son and moved in with him. Four years later the son died and du Sable's granddaughter failed to care for the older du Sable who died in 1818.

SCRIPTURE

But when the fullness of time had come, God sent his Son, born of a woman, born under the law, in order to redeem those who were under the law, so that we might receive adoption as children. And because you are children, God has sent the Spirit of his Son into our hearts, crying, "Abba! Father!" So you are no longer a slave but a child, and if a child then also an heir, through God. (Galatians 4:4–7)

PRAYER

Dear Lord, thank you for your servant Jean-Baptiste Pointe du Sable. In him we see the courage to overcome obstacles. We see you leading the way toward goodness and righting what was wrong. Help us, too, as we seek to become servants for each other and whatever is pure, right and beneficial to the gospel. Amen.

REFLECTION

In what ways are you exploring and settling your world today?

An American Woman

The awe-inspiring life of Dr. Lena Edwards can give you the chills when you truly study and read between the lines of her life to see the struggles, heartaches from oppression and discrimination as well as her insistence that all people deserve proper medical care. Hers was a saintly life that more and more people should emulate and explore.

Lena Edwards came from a strict Catholic middle-class family of Washington, D.C. Her father was a dentist and her mother was one of the founders of St. Augustine's Church in Washington. Lena went on to graduate from Howard University and then Howard University Medical School. While at Howard, she met and married Dr. Keith Madison. Lena maintained her maiden name and the couple moved from Washington to Jersey City, probably in search of integrated parochial schools.

Dr. Edwards specialized in obstetrics and gynecology. She built a thriving practice in Jersey City where she treated the poor and immigrants. While maintaining her medical practice, she had six children of her own. She remarked, "I was in a neighborhood of people from East Europe, like the Polish and the Slavish and...they were used to women, especially for maternity cases. They would come to me because they could talk freely to me. I built up a practice fairly well—very well, as a matter of fact, in spite of the fact that I was having babies one behind the other."[90] During her nearly thirty-year career in Jersey City, Dr. Edwards delivered over five thousand babies, mainly in the home, as she was an advocate for natural childbirth.

36

Dr. Lena Edwards
=====
Physician and Philanthropist

===

1900–1986

=

Even as a talented doctor, outspoken citizen and devoted mother, Lena Edwards faced many levels of discrimination due to her sex and race. She had to consistently fight for medical privileges at local hospitals and was denied residency at the local maternity hospital despite being the first national-board-certified black female obstetrician and gynecologist in the United States. Her achievements included being named one of the thirteen outstanding women doctors in 1946, a Fellow of the International College of Surgeons and Woman Doctor of the Year from the New Jersey Chapter of the American Medical Association. Still, with all of these credentials, Dr. Lena Edwards could not escape the hatred of her time. Though she could not escape, she met it with the grace and prayer that can only come from knowing the Lord.

With all of her accomplishments and awards, Dr. Lena Edwards chose to move to Hereford, Texas, to live in poverty among Mexican migrant farmworkers, joining her son, Martin Madison, a priest in the Society of the Atonement. In 1961 Dr. Edwards used her life savings plus some funds from friends in Jersey City to establish Our Lady of Guadalupe Maternity Hospital. This was her successful attempt to battle the injustice of inadequate health care for poor women.

Dr. Edwards left Texas after a heart attack but continued her medical practice in Jersey City alongside her daughter, Dr. Marie Metoyer. In 1964 President Lyndon Baines Johnson awarded Dr. Lena Edwards the Presidential Medal of Freedom. This is the highest medal awarded to civilians for service rendered to the United States. On December 3, 1986, Dr. Lena Edwards went home to God but not before making a huge impact on the lives of American citizens, rich and poor, Catholic and non-Catholic, black and white.

SCRIPTURE

"...[F]or I was hungry and you gave me food, I was thirsty and you gave me something to drink, I was a stranger and you welcomed me, I was naked and you gave me clothing, I was sick and you took care of me, I was in prison and you visited me." Then the righteous will answer him, "Lord, when was it that we saw you hungry and gave you food, or thirsty and gave you something to drink? And when was it that we saw you a stranger and welcomed you, or naked and gave you clothing? And when was it that we saw you sick or in prison and visited you?" And the king will answer them, "Truly I tell you, just as you did it to one of the least of these who are members of my family, you did it to me." (Matthew 25:35–40)

PRAYER

Dr. Lena Edwards, we cannot believe it. You gave everything away! For the sake of those in need, you spent your life savings on medical care. Really, you barely knew these people, yet no sacrifice proved too great. Providing for those in need, this is the message of the gospel. When Jesus said, "just as you did it to one of the least of these...you did it to me," you heard this redeeming message and responded without fail. We pray that we may one day hear the simple yet refreshing message of Jesus as well. Amen.

REFLECTION

How much service is enough? Is it possible to give too much? Do you have too much?

Long-Suffering Mother

Elizabeth Lange was born around 1784 , but not much is known about her before 1828 when she came to Baltimore. We know that she "came to the city of Baltimore a courageous, loving, religious woman...a strong, independent thinker and doer,"[91] according to a biography by Maria Lannon. She entered the United States in 1812 via Philadelphia from Haiti, probably accompanied by family members.

In 1828 Elizabeth Lange, Mary Frances Balas and Mary Rose Boegue came to Baltimore with the hope of forming a religious community for black women. One year later they achieved their goal and became the first successful black Catholic religious community in the U.S. (Father Charles Nerickx established the Sisters of Loretto in 1824 but the community did not survive after his death.) They were joined by Almeide Duchemin Maxis. The four professed vows to form the Oblate Sisters of Providence with a French spirituality, a devotion to Saint Benedict the Moor and a habit consisting of a black dress with white collar and large black bonnet. This black bonnet was worn outside, then replaced by the better-known white puffy bonnet with black ribbon for indoors.

The sisters faced harsh ridicule from the citizens as few saw the need for a black religious community. But the cholera epidemic of 1832 prompted authorities in Baltimore to request the sisters' assistance. Even though their mission was to educate black children, the sisters agreed to help nurse Baltimore's cholera victims. After this service, the sisters continued to face criticism and prejudice from their white

37

Mother Mary
Elizabeth Lange
=====
Religious

===

1784–1882

=

neighbors. Nevertheless, they remained faithful to their mission to educate black children.

Elizabeth Lange and her fellow Oblates willingly served and dedicated themselves unselfishly to the cause of evangelization. We know that finances remained an issue for the community and that Mother Lange gave all that she had, even the proceeds from her father's estate. After her husband's death, Lange's mother, Dede, joined the community.

A rather funny tale shows us a light and loving side to Mother Elizabeth Lange:

> [T]here was a very mischievous student in the school. She was playing tricks, sometimes frightening the younger children. One night after the silence bell, she tickled one of the younger girls. The youngster screamed aloud with lots of laughter and a little bit of fear. Everyone was disturbed. When Mother Mary called the little girl for an explanation, the child could not tell Mother the word for tickle in French, so she tickled Mother to show her. Mother Mary gathered the child in her arms, comforting her and giving her the assurance that she did indeed understand.[92]

Mother Mary Elizabeth Lange lived as an Oblate Sister of Providence for fifty-three years. She had the vision and faith to overcome the hatred and oppression of her time, as well as the internal strength to shoulder the leadership responsibilities of the young Oblate community. She died on February 3, 1882. Her cause for canonization was presented by Archbishop William Keeler of Baltimore. He described her as "a woman of faith and courage who 'set for herself and her early companions the task of teaching little ones of African descent in a culture and a climate hostile to meeting this need.'"[93]

OFFICIAL PRAYER FOR THE BEATIFICATION OF MOTHER LANGE
Almighty and Eternal God, you granted Mother Mary Lange extraordinary trust in your providence. You endowed her with humility, courage, holiness and an extraordinary sense of service to the poor and sick. You enabled her to found the Oblate Sisters of Providence and provide educational, social and spiritual ministry especially to the African American community. Mother Lange's love for all enabled her to see Christ in each person, and the pain of prejudice and racial

hatred never blurred that vision. Deign to raise her to the highest honors of the altar in order that, through her intercession, more souls may come to a deeper understanding and more fervent love of you. Heavenly Father, glorify your heart by granting also this favor (here mention your request) which we ask through the intercession of your faithful servant, Mother Mary Lange. Amen.[94]

SCRIPTURE

By contrast, the fruit of the Spirit is love, joy, peace, patience, kindness, generosity, faithfulness, gentleness, and self-control. There is no law against such things. (Galatians 5:22–23)

PRAYER

Dear daughter of Haiti, you agreed to a life of service when you brought the Oblate Sisters of Providence into existence. You and the sisters harnessed unknown energy to create a successful religious community for women of color. You did not have the needed support or the model to formulate the order but you made a way out of no way. Because of your great faith, God blessed you for this life of love and service. Dearest Mother Lange, help us to love more than we think possible. We have more love in us than we know. Amen.

REFLECTION

What are we doing to secure love and peace within our lives? With conflict, suffering and turmoil growing in our communities, what are we doing to ease the pain for ourselves and our neighbors? What does it take for a person to love and serve like Mother Lange?

A Precious Soul

38

(Dother Emma Lewis

=====

Catechist and Lay Leader

===

1868–1921

=

This wonderful woman from Philadelphia seems to have been lost in the annals of Catholic church history. At a time when black Catholics were not welcomed everywhere in Philadelphia, Emma Lewis opened her kitchen as a place for evangelization. Her critical concern was for the proper religious education of African American children.

Emma Lewis was born in Galvalease, Ohio, in 1868. She came to Philadelphia and began religious instruction with children in North Philadelphia. Archbishop Ryan of Philadelphia acknowledged her work and encouraged her to begin a mission with the financial assistance of Katharine Drexel (now Saint Katharine Drexel). Mother Emma Lewis established Our Lady of the Blessed Sacrament Mission, which later became a parish under the same name. This parish was a cornerstone for black Catholics in North Philadelphia until it closed in 1972.

Mother Lewis moved to Atlantic City in 1916 and opened another mission named St. Monica; it, too, became a parish under the supervision of the Augustinians. In 1921 Mother Emma Lewis died after many years of faithful service to the black Catholic community and the Catholic church. Her devotion to the universal church should be noted through prayer and remembrance.

SCRIPTURE

Therefore be imitators of God, as beloved children, and live in love, as Christ loved us and gave himself up for us, a fragrant offering and sacrifice to God. (Ephesians 5:1–2)

PRAYER

Mother Lewis, you held the vision and strength to establish a desperately needed mission in Philadelphia. You must have really loved the people in your care. As you evangelized the black Catholics in your home, your commitment to the community grew with the unconditional love commanded by Jesus in the Gospels. Dear mother, pray for us, that we may learn this true love for one another. Amen.

REFLECTION

How do you show others that you love them? When you say, "Hello, how are you?" do you wait for the response? Are you truly concerned with the answer or is it merely a social courtesy?

Holy Endurance

How would you feel if everyone knew who you were and your presence sometimes elicited a negative response? What would it be like to truly be alone with frustrations that no one seemed to care about? How would you exist? If you were donned with the title "The most conspicuous Man in America,"[95] how would you feel? Perhaps these few questions can lead us into the world of Father Augustus Tolton, the first African American priest in the United States.

Augustus Tolton was the second of three children born to Martha Jane Chisley and Peter Paul Tolton, both slaves on plantations in Missouri. Since both Martha Jane and Peter Paul were owned by Catholic families, they were permitted a Catholic wedding, blessed by the local priest. Their married life was difficult as they toiled in the fields and raised children. This commitment to each other brought on new trials as the Civil War raged on and slavery became an issue of the war. Many slaves answered news of the war with escape. Peter Paul Tolton was one such man who decided to fight for the Union Army. Shortly after his escape Martha Tolton fled also with her three children to Illinois, a free state.

Once settled in Quincy, Illinois, she sought a Catholic education for her children. This was yet another setback because few Catholic schools would accept black children. Her persistence paid off as Augustus and his sister, Ann (elder brother Charles was too sickly to attend school), received a limited Catholic education because they had to work in a tobacco factory to

39

Father Augustus Tolton
=====
Priest

===

1854–1897

=

help support the family. During this time, Augustus spent time as a Sunday school teacher and had the opportunity to interact with very supportive Franciscan priests who taught him Latin, Greek, German, English and a host of other subjects. When Augustus expressed a desire to become a priest, the two pastors in Quincy came to his aid.

Because of constant rejections by seminaries in the United States, Augustus entered Urban College in Rome to prepare for the priesthood. Originally, he was preparing for African missions, but this plan was altered. Tolton often spoke about this plan of God for him:

> I heard the words of St. John "prepare the ways of the Lord" and God gave me the strength to persevere.... I rejoyced [sic] when I heard that I was [to] be sent to America. God is over us all, and has many blessings for men of every race.... It was said that I would be the only priest of my race in America and would not be likely to succeed. All at once Cardinal Simoni [sic] said, "America has been called the most enlightened nation; we will see if it deserves that honor. If America has never seen a black priest, it has to see one now."[96]

After his ordination in 1886 Tolton arrived back in the United States to say his first Mass in Hoboken, New Jersey, at St. Mary's Hospital. He traveled back to Quincy, Illinois, to begin his pastorship at St. Joseph, an all-black parish. But it was not long before white Catholics from neighboring parishes began coming to Father Tolton for Mass and to receive sacramental preparation. This, of course, angered his brother priests who did not understand the attraction of Father Tolton. Their own hatred and inability to see the appeal caused severe hardship upon this lonely Catholic priest.

These conditions intensified in November of 1887 as Father Michael Weiss began as pastor of St. Boniface Church in Quincy. Father Weiss was appointed as the head of the Qunicy-area Catholic clergy. In this role he did not like white Catholics attending Mass with Father Tolton and voiced his displeasure by calling Father Tolton "that nigger priest."[97] He also convinced their bishop to order Father Tolton to "desist from luring white worshippers and...to minister to Negro people only or to go elsewhere."[98] Their thought also concerned white Catholics giving financial support to this black church.

If white Catholics had any financial reserves, they belonged in white churches, not black, as the thinking went. Roy Bauer in *They Called Him Father Gus* tells this story:

> Another incident in 1889 put Father Tolton in an unacceptable light with some in Quincy. A wealthy, Catholic, white, society matron's daughter planned to marry an "unacceptable" person. The mother put the pressure on the priests in town to close their doors to her daughter. However, she forgot about Father Tolton. When the couple asked Father Gus to officiate at their wedding in St. Joseph Church, he obtained, very quietly, the permission of her pastor and proceeded with the wedding.[99]

After this event, Father Tolton had to leave Illinois. There was no forgiving his support of this interracial marriage taking place in a black church. On December 19, 1889, Father Augustus Tolton left for Chicago. He became pastor of St. Mary's Church, Chicago's first black church and known as a sub-parish as it was located in the basement of St. Mary's Church where white Catholics worshiped.

Before he could afford a rectory, Father Tolton lived in a one-room apartment alone. Soon his mother, sister and some parishioners from Quincy joined him in Chicago. Though this lightened his concern about loneliness, he still shouldered the burden of his small parish alone. Often he wrote to Mother Katharine Drexel in Bensalem, Pennsylvania, for assistance. In 1893 he wrote:

> I have altogether 260 souls to render an account of before God's majesty. There [are] altogether 500 souls but they have become like unto the dead limbs on a tree and without moisture because no one had taken care of them: just Sunday night last I was called to the death bed of a colored woman who had been 9 years away from her duties because she was hurled out of a white church and even cursed at by the Irish members, very bad indeed! She sent for me and thanked God that she had one [a black priest] to send for.[100]

This was an enthusiastic letter expressing his vision for the small community in his care. His attitude would change shortly as funds ran out and his health declined. In another letter to Mother Katharine, Father

Tolton said, "They watch us, just the same as the Pharisees did our Lord,"[101] referring to being the first black Catholic priest in America.

Augustus Tolton died on July 9, 1897, from the overbearing summer heat of Illinois. He was forty-three years old and had spent eleven years as a priest serving God's people in poverty and humility.

SCRIPTURE

Now as an elder myself and a witness of the sufferings of Christ, as well as one who shares in the glory to be revealed, I exhort the elders among you to tend the flock of God that is in your charge, exercising the oversight, not under compulsion but willingly, as God would have you do it—not for sordid gain but eagerly. (1 Peter 5:1–2)

PRAYER

Father Augustus Tolton, our community loves you! The untiring and self-sacrificing energy that you gave to the church cannot be forgotten or ignored. You must be a champion in heaven for what you did for the people in your care. Although your brother priests refused to assist you, history reveals their loss and your love for the church. Dear Father Tolton, pray for us; help us to love each other despite our fears, despite our loneliness, despite weariness and frustrations. You lived with enough of these conditions but continued to build up the body of Christ here on earth. May your life strengthen us all. Amen.

REFLECTION

How easy is it for you to quit when things are frustratingly harsh? When do you allow fear and loneliness to overtake you? In times like these, what can you do?

Faithful Sister

When the question is asked, "Who are these handmaids?" the answer must always begin with the life of Mother Mary Theodore Williams. The Franciscan Handmaids of the Most Pure Heart of Mary was established in 1917 by Mother Mary Theodore Williams (born Elizabeth Barbara Williams) with the support and encouragement of Reverend Ignatius Lisser, S.M.A. (Society of African Missions). Father Lisser approached Mother Williams in response to a proposed bill by the state of Georgia that would prohibit white teachers from instructing African American children. He clearly saw a need for African American teachers to maintain educational opportunities for black children.

Mother Williams agreed to the challenge of establishing this new community as she was waiting for the response to her daily question, "Lord, what would you have me to do?" She had already experienced religious life in a suppressed community and more recently as an Oblate Sister of Providence. According to their mission statement, the Handmaids strive "to serve one another and those committed to their care with the same care, diligence, zeal and love as Our Blessed Lady served her Divine Son."[102]

The Handmaids experienced the harshness of the American South as they attempted to pursue their educational mission for black children. They were faced with extreme discrimination and negativity that eventually forced them to leave Savannah, Georgia, in favor of Harlem, New York, to establish a day nursery there. Although this was not their mission, the small community opted for the change rather than possibly face suppression at a later date.

The parents in Harlem were overjoyed when the sisters arrived and St. Benedict Day

40

Mother Mary Theodore
Williams

=====

Religious

===

1868–1931

=

Nursery became the first Catholic day nursery in Harlem. This led the sisters to their next milestone of fulfilling their mission, as the parents wanted their children educated after they completed their time at St. Benedict Day Nursery. Therefore, St. Mary's Primary School was opened to meet this need.

In New York the sisters faced some of the same prejudice as in the South as no one fully accepted black religious, even in the North. Just to survive, the sisters were often forced to take in laundry and beg for food (for themselves and the poor in their care). This manner of living eventually took its toll on Mother Theodore as she died of pneumonia in 1931. Her prayerful spirit and unyielding work ethic caused the Handmaids to become a stable and contributing religious community to the citizens of Harlem, New York, where they are still active today and still running St. Benedict Day Nursery.

Who indeed are these handmaids?

We see ourselves with a vital role in the great task of evangelization, particularly among our African American brothers and sisters. Our role is also to witness to the world that Christ came for all men and women regardless of race. We strive to be instruments of peace, and to achieve the Handmaids ideal..."to serve one another and those committed to their care with the same diligence, zeal and love as our Blessed Lady served her Divine Son."[103]

SCRIPTURE

[J]ust as I try to please everyone in everything I do, not seeking my own advantage, but that of many, so that they may be saved. (1 Corinthians 10:33)

PRAYER

Dear Mother Theodore, your vocation was to educate children. How marvelous that you accepted change by moving to New York and opening the day nursery. How did you know that God was working for you? Because of your sacrifice, the people of Harlem were blessed. Help us as we go through the constant changes in our own lives.

REFLECTION

Sometimes we need to change plans to yield a better result. How do we react when our best laid plans fall apart? What could we do if we were not afraid of change?

Appendix A
Calendar of Selected Saints

JANUARY

17   Saint Antony of Egypt
20   Blessed Cyprian Michael Iwene Tansi

FEBRUARY

8   Saint Josephine Bakhita
28   Martyrs of the Alexandrian Plague

MARCH

7   Saints Felicitas and Perpetua

APRIL

2   Saint Mary of Egypt
4   Saint Benedict the Moor

MAY

3   Saints Timothy and Maura
22   Saint Julia of Carthage

JUNE

3   Saint Charles Lwanga and Companions
30   Venerable Pierre Toussaint

JULY

17   Saint Speratus and Companions
28   Pope Saint Victor I

AUGUST

15   Blesssed Isidore Bakanja
21   Blessed Victoria Rasomanarivo
26   Saint Serapion the Sendanite
27   Saint Monica
27   Saint Poemen
28   Saint Augustine
28   Saint Moses the Black

SEPTEMBER

    16   Saint Cyprian of Carthage

    22   Saint Maurice and the Theban Legion

OCTOBER

    8   Saint Thais

    18–20   Blesseds Daudi Okelo and Jildo Irwa

NOVEMBER

    3   Saint Martin de Porres

    21   Pope Saint Gelasius I

DECEMBER

    1   Blessed Marie Clementine Anuarite Nengapeta

    3   Saint Cassian of Tangier

    6   Blessed Theresa Chikaba

    10   Pope Saint Militiades

Appendix B
Litany of African Saints

Lord, in your great wisdom and mercy, you sent the world these holy men and women to embrace us, to nurture us, love us, intercede for us and walk with us. We humbly thank you and pray:

Lord, have mercy on us.
> Christ, have mercy on us.

Lord, have mercy on us.

Christ, hear us.
> Christ, graciously hear us.

Holy Mary, Mother of God, Pray for us.
(repeat the phrase "Pray for us" after each name)

Saint Aaron
Saint Abadias
Saint Abadiu
Saint Abakerazum
Saint Abakuh
Saint Abeluzius
Saints Aberah and Atom
Saint Abhar
Saint Abibus
Saints Abibus and Sabinus
Saints Abidianus and Quirinus and
    147 Companions
Saint Abilius
Saint Ablak
Saint Abnodius
Saint Abraham the Poor
Saints Abraham and John
Saint Abraham
Saint Abrahman
Saints Abrah and Atzheha
Saint Absadah
Saints Acaubi and Companions
Saint Accidia

Saint Acha
Saint Achatius
Saint Achillas
Saint Achilleus
Saint Acra
Saint Acronius
Saint Acutus
Saint Acutus and Companions
Saint Adelphius
Saint Adeodatus
Saint Adjutor and Companions
Saint Adjutor
Saint Adjutus
Saint Adramas
Saint Adrian of Canterbury
Saint Adrianus and Companions
Saints Adrianus, Victurus and
    Secundilla
Saint Aizan
Saints Aizan and Sazan
Saint Andrianicus
Saints Adrion, Victor and Basilla
Saints Aedeses and Applianus

Saint Aemilianus
Saint Aemilius and Companions
Saint Aemilius
Saints Aemilius and Castus
Saint Aethiops
African Martyrs
Saint Africanus
Alexandrian Plague Martyrs
Saint Ampelius
Saint Antiochus
Martyrs of Antinoe
Saint Antoninus
Saint Antoninus
Saint Anthony
Saint Anthony
Saint Anthony
Saint Anthony the Great of Thebes
Saint Anurite
Saint Anub
Saint Anub
Saint Apali
Saint Apalion
Saint Apamon
Saint Apalles
Saint Aphrodidius
Saint Aphodidius
Saint Aphodidius
Saint Apollinaris
Saint Apollinaris
Saint Apollo
Saint Apollo the Solitary
Saint Apollo(Apolonuis)
Saint Apollo
Saint Apollo
Saint Apollo
Saint Apollonis
Saint Apollonius (with Philemon)
Saint Apollonius
Saint Apollonius
Saint Apollonius
Saint Apollonius
Saint Appianus
Saint Aprax
Saint Aprillis

Saint Aptil
Saint Aquilinus
Saint Aradus
Saint Aradus
Saint Archelaus
Saint Archimmus of Mascula
Saint Arcadius
Saint Archildes
Saint Ares
Saint Michael Argave
Saint Armogastes and Companions
Saint Artemius
Saint Asclas
Saint Athanasius of Alexandria
Saint Athganasius Badzekuketta
Saint Athanasius and Companions
Saint Augustine
Saint Aurelius
Saint Avitus

Saint Josephine Bakhita
Blessed Isidore Bakanja
Saint Joseph Mukasa Balikuddembe
Saint Luke Banabakintu
Saint Basilides
Saints Bassa, Paula and Protalicus
Saint Athanasius Bazzeketta
Saint Benedict the Moor
Saint Benjamin
Saint Bessarion
Saint Blasius
Saint Boniface and Thecla
Saint Bruno Serankuma
Saint James Buzabaliawo

Saint Caecilius
Saint Caesarius
Saint John Cassian
Saint Cassian of Tangier
Saint Castor
Saint Castus and Aemelius
Saint Catherine of Labourne
Saint Catherine of Alexandria
Saint Cecilius

Saint Cerbonius, Bishop of
  Papalonius
Saints Chaermon and Ischyrian
Saints Chrysanthus and Doria
Venerable Teresa Chikaba
Saint Crispina
Saints Currentius, Timothy, Saldia,
  Felicianus and Juncundus
Saint Cyprian of Carthage
Blessed Cyprian Michael Tansi
Saints Cyprain, Felix and 4,966
  Confessors
Saint Cyril of Alexandria
Saints Cyrus and John

Blesseds Daudi Okelo and Jildo Irwa
Saint Dativus
Saint Demetrius, Bishop of
  Alexandria
Saint Deogratias
Saints Didymium and Theodora
Saint Dionysius, Bishop of
  Alexandria
Saint Dioscorus of Alexandria
Saints Donatian, Laetus, Mansuetus,
  Germanus, Presides and
  Fusculus
Saint Dorotheus of Thebes
Saint Dulas the Patient
Saints Elesbaan, Aretas and Martyrs
  of Najran
Saint Elias
Saint Elias the Eunuch
Saints Elias, Jeremy, Isias, Samuel
  and Daniel
Saint Emeritus
Saints Epimachus and Alexander
Saint Eugene the Copt
Saint Eugenius of Carthage
Saint Euprasia
Saint Evagrius Ponticus

Saint Fabianus and Companions
Saint Felix
Saint Felix of Thibuica

Saint Frumentius
Saint Fulgentius

Saint Gelasius I, Pope
Blessed Abba Ghebre Michael
Saint Gonzaga Gonza

Saint Heraclas
Saint Hyperechius

Saint Ingenes
Saint Isaac
Saint Isaac
Saint Isaac the Just
Saint Isaias of Scete
Saint Isadore
Saint Isadore of Chios
Saint Isadore of Pelusium
Saint Isadore of Alexandris
Saint John the Almsgiver
Saints John, Andrew and
  Theophilus
Saint John the Dwarf
Saint John of Egypt
Saint John the Physician
Saint Joseph (Coptic Saint)
Saint Joseph Analytinus
Saint Joseph (Egyptian)
Saint Joseph, son of Photina
Saint Joseph
Saint Joseph
Saint Joseph, Coptic Patriarch of
  Alexandria

Saint Julia of Carthage
Saints Julian and Basilissa
Saints Julian, Cronion and Besas
Saint Julianus and Companions
Saint Julianus
Saint Julius of Acfahs

Saint Andrew Kaggwa
Saint Matthias Kalemba
Saint Ambrose Kibuka
Saint Anatole Kiriggwajjo
Saint Kizito

Saint Mukasa Kiriwawanvu
Saint Achilles Kiwanuka

Saint Lalibala
Saint Leonides
Saint Liberatus
Saint Longinus
Saint Lucius
Saint Lucius of Cyrene
Saint Adolphus Mukasa Ludigo
Saint Charles Lwanga

Saint Macarius of Alexandria
Saint Macarius the Elder
Saint Macarius the Younger
Saint Mappaticus
Saint Marcellinus
Saint Marcellinus
Saint Marcellinus and Companions
Saint Marcellus the centurian
Saint Marciana, Virgin Martyr of
    Mauritania
Saint Marcus
Saints Marion and James
Saint Mark the Rich
Saint Mark the Faster
Saint Martin de Porres
Saint Mary
Saint Mary of Egypt
Saint Maurice of Aganaum and
    Companions
Saint Maximilian
Saints Meleus, Trophonius, Mortialis
    and Silvanus
Saint Menas
Saint Menas, Patriarch of
    Constantinople
Saint Metras
Saint Militiades, Pope
Saint Monica
Saints Montanus, Lucius and
    Companions
Saint Moses the Black
Saint Mugagga
Saint Jean-Marie Muzeyi

Saint Myrope
Saint Noe Mwahhali

Saint Najran Martyrs
Saint Nemesian and Companions
Saint Nemesius and Companions
Saint Nennas
Saint Pontian Ngondwe

Saint Onuphrius
Saint Optatus of Melevis
Saint Orsiesius

Saint Pachomius
Saint Palaemon
Saint Paladius
Saint Pambo
Saint Pantaenus
Saint Paul the Hermit
Saint Paul the Simple
Saint Peleus, Nilus and Companions
Saints Perpetua and Felicitas
Saint Peter of Alexandria
Saint Phileas of Thmius
Saint Pierius
Saints Plutarch, Potamiana and
    Companions
Saint Poemen
Saint Pompejus
Saint Ponephysis
Saint Pontius
Saint Porphyrius
Saint Possidius
Saint Possedonius
Saint Possessor
Saint Possessor
Saint Postumia
Saint Potomon
Saint Proterius
Saint Ptolemy

Saint Quintas

Saint Raissa
Saint Regulus
Saint Restituta

Saint Revocatus
Saint Rogatian

Saint Sara
Saint Sarmata
Saints Saturninus, Dativus and
    Companions
Saint Schenute
Saint Serapion of Arsenoe
Martyrs of Serapion
Saint Serapion the Scholastic
Saint Serapion the Sendanite
Saint Bruno Serunkuma
Saint Servanus and Companions
Saint Shenuf and His Brothers
Saint Shenusi
Saint Silvanus
Saint Simon of Cyrene
Saint Simon Salus
Saint Sistoes the Hermit
Saint Denis Ssebuggwawo
Saint Stephanie
Saint Synclitica

Saint Tekkla
Saint Thais
Saint Thelica
Saints Theodora and Didymus
Saint Theodora of Alexandria
Saint Theodore, Bishop of Egypt
Saint Theodore, Forty-First
    Patriarch of Alexandria
Saint Theodore, Bishop Martyr
Saint Theodore of Cyrene
Saints Theodore, Timothy and
    Calliopius
Saint Theodore the Sanctified
Saint Theophilius and Companions
Saints Timothy and Maura
Saint Timothy I
Saint Timothy II
Saint Timothy III
Saint Tipasius
Venerable Pierre Toussaint

Saint Tryphon, Cyrion and
    Companions
Saint Turana
The Turabatan Martyrs
Saint Mbaga Tuzinde
The Twelve Brothers
Saints Tyrannio, Zenobius and
    Companions
Saint Tyria
Saint Tytirus
Saint Tzabala Mariam
Saint Tzanas

Martyrs of Utica
Saints Urbanus, Victor and
    Companions
Saint Urbanus and Forty
    Companions
Saint Urbanus, fifth-century bishop
Saints Ursus and Catulinus
Saints Ursus and Victor

Saints Valerianus, Urbanus and
    Companions
Saints Valerius, Rufinus and
    Companions
Saint Variacus
Saint Venusta
Saint Venustus
Saint Varus
Saint Valentine
Saints Valentine and Dubatatus
Saints Valeria and Anesius
Saint Valerian
Saint Vicentis
Saint Victor, Ethiopian Prince
Saint Victor Maurus
Saint Victor, Bishop of Vita
Saint Victor, priest, martyr of
    Carthage
Saint Victor the Ninivite
Saint Victor
Saints Victor, Dacius and Irene
Saint Victor
Saint Victor, Pope

Saint Victoria
Saint Victoria
Saint Victoria
Blessed Victoria Rasomarivo
Saint Victorian
Saint Victorianus
Saint Victorianus
Saint Victorinus and Companions
Saint Victorius
Saint Victorurus
Saint Victurus and Companions
Saint Victurus
Saint Vindanius
Saints Vindemialis of Capsa and
  Longinus
Saint Vindemialis and Companions
Saint Vindemials
Saint Visa
Saint Vitalis
Saint Vitus
Saint Volutianus

Saint Xystus

Saint Yeshak
Saint Yostema

Saint Zabarias
Saint Zacchaeus
Saint Zacchaeus

Saints Zacchaeus and Theodore
Saint Zaccaharias the Abyssinian
Saint Zaccharias
Saint Zaccharias
Saints Zaccharias and Cassius
Saint Zaccharias
Saint Zacharias
Saint Zacharias the Ethiopian
Saint Zaina
Saint Za-Jysus
Saint Za-Michael
Saint Zanurius
Saint Zara Abraham
Saint Zara Jacob
Saint Zaticus
Saint Zaticus and Companions
Saint Zaticus and Companions
Saint Zeno and Companions
Saint Zeno, martyr
Saint Zeno, warrior, martyr
Saint Zeno, fourth-century
  Anchorite
Saint Zeno Alexandrian Martyr
Saint Ziddenus
Saint Zitus and Companions
Saint Zina
Saint Zophorus
Saint Zozimus[104]

Appendix C
Map of Modern-Day Africa

Bibliography

BOOKS

Attwater, Donald. *Martyrs: From St. Stephen to John Tung.* New York: Sheed and Ward, 1957.

Augustine, Saint. *Confessions.* Henry Chadwick, trans. New York: Oxford University Press, 1992.

Ball, Ann. *Faces of Holiness.* Huntington, Ind.: Our Sunday Visitor, 1998.

———. *Modern Saints: Their Lives and Faces.* vols. 1–2. Rockford, Ill.: Tan, 1983.

Bauer, Roy. *They Called Him Father Gus: The Life and Times of Augustine Tolton, First Black Priest in the U.S.A.* Quincy, Ill.: Quincy University Press, 1999.

Brown, S.J., Joseph A. *A Retreat With Thea Bowman and Bede Abram: Leaning on the Lord.* Cincinnati: St. Anthony Messenger, 1997.

Cepress, F.S.P.A., Celestine, ed. *Sister Thea Bowman: Shooting Star: Selected Writings and Speeches.* Winona, Minn.: St. Mary's / Christian Brothers, 1993.

Collins, David R. *Servant to the Slaves: The Story of Henriette Delille.* Boston: Pauline, 2000.

Cristiani, Leon. *Saint Monica and Her Son Augustine.* Boston: Pauline, 1977.

Dagnino, Maria Luisa. *Bakhita: A Song of Freedom.* Rome: Canossiane Figlie della Carità, 2000.

———. *Bakhita Tells Her Story.* Rome: Canossiane Figlie della Carità, 1993.

Davis, O.S.B., Cyprian. *The History of Black Catholics in the United States.* New York: Crossroad, 1990.

DeDomenico, F.S.P., Elizabeth Marie. *Saint Martin de Porres: Humble Healer.* Boston: Pauline, 2005.

Fanning, M.H.M., James. *Clementine Anuarite.* Africa: St. Paul, 1987.

Faupel, J.F. *African Holocaust: The Story of the Uganda Martyrs.* Africa: St. Paul, 1984.

Hanley, O.F.M., Boniface. *Ten Christians.* Notre Dame, Ind.: Ave Maria, 1979.

Holtzclaw, R. Fulton. *The Saints Go Marching In: A One Volume Hagiography of Africans, or Descendants of Africans, Who Have Been Canonized by the Church, Including Three of the Early Popes.* Shaker Heights, Oh.: Keeble, 1984.

Lannon, Maria M. *Response to Love: The Story of Mother Mary Elizabeth Lange.* Washington, D.C.: Josephite Pastoral Center, 1992.

Mohler, James A. *Late Have I Loved You: An Interpretation of Saint Augustine on Human and Divine Relationships.* New York: New City, 1991.

Monahan, Joan. *Martin de Porres: A Saint for Our Time.* Mahwah, N.J.: Paulist, 2002.

Morrow, Diane Batts. *Persons of Color and Religious at the Same Time: The Oblate Sisters of Providence, 1828-1860.* Chapel Hill, N.C.: The University of North Carolina Press, 2002.

Musurillo, Herbert, trans. *The Acts of the Christian Martyrs.* Oxford: Oxford University Press, 1972.

New Catholic Encyclopedia, second edition, vols. 4, 6. Thomson Gale, 2002.

O'Brien, Felicity. *Saints in the Making.* Dublin: Veritas, 1988.

O'Malley, C.M., Vincent J. *Saints of Africa.* Huntington, Ind.: Our Sunday Visitor, 2001.

Quinn, Frederick. *African Saints: Saints, Martyrs, and Holy People from the Continent of Africa.* New York: Crossroad, 2002.

Tarry, Ellen. *Pierre Toussaint: Apostle of Old New York.* Boston: Pauline, 1998.

Salisbury, Joyce. *Perpetua's Passion: The Death and Memory of a Young Roman Woman.* New York: Routledge, 1997.

Thurston, S.J., Herbert, and Donald Attwater, eds. *Butler's Lives of the Saints: Complete Edition,* vols. 1, 2, 3. New York: P.J. Kenedy and Sons, 1956.

Trickey-Bapty, Carolyn. *Martyrs and Miracles: The Inspiring Lives of Saints and Martyrs.* New York: Testament, 2001.

Ward, S.L.G., Benedicta, trans. *The Desert Fathers: Sayings of the Early Christian Monks.* New York: Penguin, 2003.

———. *The Sayings of the Desert Fathers: The Alphabetical Collection.* Kalamazoo, Mich.: Cistercian, 1975.

BROCHURE

The Franciscan Handmaids of the Most Pure Heart of Mary. "Who Are These Handmaids." New York: The Franciscan Handmaids of Mary Motherhouse.

NEWSPAPER ARTICLES

Brinkmann, Susan. "Relying on Providence: Mother Mary Elizabeth Lange." *The Catholic Standard and Times.* February 16, 2006.

"Colored Priest Rev. A. Derricks, Trinitarian, Dies." *The Catholic Standard and Times.* Philadelphia, November 2, 1929.

"Rev. Augustus Tolton, The most conspicuous Man in America" *American Catholic Tribune.* March 11, 1887.

WEB SITES

Georgia Women of Achievement. "Mathilda Taylor Beasley." http://www.georgia-women.org/_honorees/beasleym/index.htm.

Justpeace. "Henriette Delille...." http://www.justpeace.org/henriette.htm.

New Jersey City University. "Lena Frances Edwards, MD, 1900-1986." http://www.njcu.edu/programs/jchistory/Pages/E_Pages/Edwards_Lena.htm.

Pope John Paul II. "Mass for the Beatification of Father Cyprian Tansi." The Vatican. http://www.vatican.va/holy_father/john_paul_ii/travels/documents/hf_jp-ii_hom_22031998_nigeria-beatification_en.html.

The Vatican. "Biography: Daudi Okelo and Jildo Irwa." http://www.pcf.va/news_services/liturgy/saints/ns_lit_doc_20021020_okelo-irwa_en.html.

VIDEOCASSETTE

Sr. Thea: Her Own Story. Washington, D.C.: United States Catholic Conference Oblate Media and Communication Campaign, 1988.

Notes

1. Cyprian Davis, O.S.B., *The History of Black Catholics in the United States* (New York: Crossroads, 1990), p. 16.
2. Carolyn Trickey-Bapty, *Martyrs and Miracles: The Inspiring Lives of Saints and Martyrs* (New York: Testament, 2001), p. 90.
3. Herbert Thurston, S.J., and Donald Attwater, eds., *Butler's Lives of the Saints: Complete Edition*, vol. 1 (New York: P.J. Kenedy and Sons, 1956), p. 437.
4. Donald Attwater, *Martyrs: From St. Stephen to John Tung* (New York: Sheed and Ward, 1957), pp. 48–49.
5. Benedicta Ward, S.L.G., trans., *The Desert Fathers: Sayings of the Early Christian Monks* (New York: Penguin, 2003), p. 3.
6. Ward, p. 3.
7. Ward, p. 53.
8. Ward, p. 88.
9. Ward, p. 148.
10. Robert Fulton Holtzclaw, *The Saints Go Marching In: A One Volume Hagiography of Africans, or Descendants of Africans, Who Have Been Canonized by the Church, Including Three of the Early Popes* (Shaker Heights, Oh.: Keeble, 1984), p. 26.
11. Saint Augustine, *Confessions*, Henry Chadwick, trans. (New York: Oxford University Press, 1992), Book V, chap. iv, para. 7, p. 75.
12. Saint Augustine, *Confessions*, Book II, chap. iii, para. 7, p. 27.
13. Saint Augustine, *Confessions*, Book III, chap. i, para. 1, p. 35.
14. Saint Augustine, *Confessions*, Book III, chap. v, para. 9, p. 40.
15. Saint Augustine, *Confessions*, Book VIII, chap. xii, para. 29, p. 152.
16. Saint Augustine, *Confessions*, Book X, chap. xxvii, para. 27, p. 201.
17. Leon Cristiani, *Saint Monica and Her Son Augustine*, M. Angeline Bouchard, trans. (Boston: Pauline, 1977), p. 97.
18. Saint Augustine, *Confessions*, Book I, chap. i, para. 1, p. 3.
19. Ann Ball, *Faces of Holiness: Modern Saints in Photos and Words* (Huntington, Ind.: Our Sunday Visitor, 1998), p. 126.
20. Ball, p. 126.
21. Ball, p. 125.
22. Pope John Paul II, speech during 1980 trip to Zaire, as quoted in Ball, pp. 128–129.
23. Maria Luisa Dagnino, *Bakhita: A Song of Freedom* (Rome: Canossiane Figlie della Carità, 2000), p. 68.
24. Maria Luisa Dagnino, *Bakhita Tells Her Story* (Rome: Canossiane Figlie della Carità, 1993), p. 36.
25. Dagnino, *Bakhita Tells Her Story*, pp. 62, 63.
26. Dagnino, *Bakhita Tells Her Story*, p. 71.
27. Dagnino, *Bakhita Tells Her Story*, p. 70.
28. Dagnino, *Bakhita: A Song of Freedom*, p. 65.

29. Herbert Thurston and Donald Attwater, eds., *Butler's Lives of the Saints: Complete Edition,* vol. 2 (New York: P.J. Kenedy and Sons, 1956), pp. 30–31.
30. *New Catholic Encyclopedia,* second edition, vol. 4 (Thomson Gale, 2002), p. 457.
31. Attwater, p. 39.
32. Attwater, p. 199.
33. Pope Paul VI, speech during 1969 trip to Uganda, as quoted in J.F. Faupel, *African Holocaust: The Story of the Ugandan Martyrs* (Africa: St. Paul, 1962), pp. 224, 225.
34. See Joan Monahan, *Martin de Porres: A Saint for Our Time* (Mahwah, N.J.: Paulist, 2002), pp. 31–32.
35. Monahan, p. 26.
36. Elizabeth Marie DeDomenico, F.S.P., *Saint Martin de Porres: Humble Healer* (Boston: Pauline, 2005), p. 80.
37. Monahan, pp. 72–74.
38. Holtzclaw, p. 106.
39. Herbert Thurston and Donald Attwater, eds., *Butler's Lives of the Saints: Complete Edition,* vol. 3 (New York: P.J. Kenedy and Sons, 1956), p. 619.
40. Holtzclaw, pp. 109–110.
41. Saint Augustine, *Confessions,* Book IX, chap. viii, para. 18, p. 167.
42. Cristiani, p. 23.
43. Cristiani, p. 34.
44. Cristiani, p. 33.
45. Cristiani, p. 35.
46. Saint Augustine, *Confessions,* Book IX, chap. x, para. 26, p. 172.
47. Saint Augustine, *Confessions,* Book IX, chap. xii, para. 29, p. 174.
48. Saint Augustine, *Confessions,* Book IX, chap. xii, para. 33, p. 176.
49. Thurston and Attwater, *Butler's Lives of the Saints,* vol. 3, pp. 435–436.
50. Benedicta Ward, S.L.G., *The Sayings of the Desert Fathers* (Kalamazoo, Mich.: Cistercian, 1984), pp. 138–139.
51. James Fanning, M.H.M., *Clementine Anuarite* (Africa: St. Paul, 1987), p. 30.
52. Fanning, p. 35.
53. Fanning, p. 40.
54. Fanning, pp. 41–42.
55. Herbert Musurillo, trans., *The Acts of the Christian Martyrs* (Oxford: Oxford University Press, 1972), p. 109.
56. Musurillo, p. 109.
57. Musurillo, p. 111.
58. Attwater, pp. 28–29.
59. The Vatican, "Biography: Daudi Okelo and Jildo Irwa," http://www.pcf.va/news_services/liturgy/saints/ns_lit_doc_20021020_okelo-irwa_en.html.

60. The Vatican, "Biography: Daudi Okelo and Jildo Irwa," http://www.pcf.va/news_services/liturgy/saints/ns_lit_doc_20021020_okel o-irwa_en.html.

61. The Vatican, "Biography: Daudi Okelo and Jildo Irwa," http://www.pcf.va/news_services/liturgy/saints/ns_lit_doc_20021020_okel o-irwa_en.html.

62. Ward, *The Desert Fathers*, p. 5.

63. Ward, *The Desert Fathers*, p. 5.

64. Ward, *The Desert Fathers*, p. 5.

65. Ward, *The Desert Fathers*, p. 25.

66. Ward, *The Desert Fathers*, p. 81.

67. Ward, *The Desert Fathers*, p. 85.

68. Ward, *The Desert Fathers*, p. 85.

69. Ward, *The Desert Fathers*, p. 135.

70. Ward, *The Desert Fathers*, p. 173.

71. Felicity O'Brien, *Saints in the Making* (Dublin: Veritas, 1988), p. 63.

72. O'Brien, p. 69.

73. Thurston and Attwater, *Butler's Lives of the Saints,* vol. 3, p. 125.

74. Attwater, pp. 19–20.

75. As quoted in Frederick Quinn, *African Saints: Saints, Martyrs, and Holy People from the Continent of Africa* (New York: Crossroad, 2002), p. 183.

76. As quoted in Quinn, p. 183.

77. Pope John Paul II, "Mass for the Beatification of Father Cyprian Tansi," The Vatican, http://www.vatican.va/holy_father/john_paul_ii/travels/doc-uments/hf_jp-ii_hom_22031998_nigeria-beatification_en.html.

78. Holtzclaw, p. 150.

79. Boniface Hanley, O.F.M., *Ten Christians* (Notre Dame, Ind.: Ave Maria, 1979), p. 21.

80. The Vatican is currently investigating a possibility, a little boy cured of curvature of the spine. To report a miracle, contact The Pierre Toussaint Guild, 1011 First Ave., Room 1315, New York, NY, 10022.

81. As quoted in Georgia Women of Achievement, "Mathilda Taylor Beasley," http://www.georgiawomen.org/_honorees/beasleym/index.htm.

82. As quoted in Davis, p. 111.

83. Mathilda Taylor Beasley's obituary, *The Savannah Morning News,* December 21, 1903, as quoted in Georgia Women of Achievement, "Mathilda Taylor Beasley," http://www.georgiawomen.org/_honorees/beasleym/index.htm.

84. *Sr. Thea: Her Own Story,* VHS, directed by Aaron Mermelstein (Washington, D.C.: United States Catholic Conference/Oblate Media and Communication Campaign, 1988).

85. Thea Bowman, *Sister Thea Bowman, Shooting Star: Selected Writings and Speeches,* Celestine Cepress, F.S.P.A., Ph.D., ed. (Winona, Minn.: St. Mary's / Christian Brothers, 1993), p. 32.

86. David R. Collins, *Servant to the Slaves: The Story of Henriette Delille* (Boston: Pauline, 2000), p. 62.

87. Justpeace, "Henriette Delille...," http://www.justpeace.org/henriette.htm.

88. "Colored Priest, Rev. A. Derricks, Trinitarian, Dies," *The Catholic Standard and Times*, Philadelphia, November 2, 1929.

89. "Colored Priest, Rev. A. Derricks, Trinitarian, Dies,"*The Catholic Standard and Times*.

90. Linda Janet Holmes, "The Life of Lena Edwards, 1900-1986," *New Jersey Medicine*, May 1988, pp. 431–435, as quoted in New Jersey City University, "Lena Frances Edwards, MD, 1900-1986," http://www.njcu.edu/programs/jchistory/Pages/E_Pages/Edwards_Lena.htm.

91. Maria M. Lannon, *Response to Love: The Story of Mother Mary Elizabeth Lange, O.S.P.* (Washington, D.C.: Josephite Pastoral Center, 1992), p. 3.

92. Lannon, p. 9.

93. Susan Brinkmann, "Relying on Providence: Mother Mary Elizabeth Lange," *The Catholic Standard and Times*, Philadelphia, February 16, 2006, p. 7.

94. Brinkmann, p. 7. If favors received, please contact the Oblate Sisters of Providence at 401-242-8500.

95. *American Catholic Tribune*, March 11, 1887.

96. Speech by Augustus Tolton, as quoted in Davis, p. 155.

97. Roy Bauer, *They Called Him Father Gus: The life and times of Augustine Tolton, First Black Priest in the U.S.A.* (Quincy, Ill.: Quincy University Press, 1999), p. 21.

98. Bauer, p. 22.

99. Bauer, pp. 22–23.

100. Davis, p. 159.

101. Davis, p. 161.

102. "Who Are These Handmaids," (New York: The Franciscan Handmaids of Mary Motherhouse), p. 13.

103. "Who Are These Handmaids," p. 13.

104. This is a list of Catholic saints attributed to the continent of Africa. Although many argue there is proof that only a few from this list were actually people of color and we do not know for certain who was black-skinned, ethnically mixed or simply a European living on the continent, our primary concern is to remember that people of African descent have been canonized by the Catholic church.

Index